THE POWER AND VALUE OF
PHILOSOPHICAL SKEPTICISM

THE POWER AND VALUE OF PHILOSOPHICAL SKEPTICISM

Jeffrey P. Whitman

ROWMAN & LITTLEFIELD PUBLISHERS, INC.

ROWMAN & LITTLEFIELD PUBLISHERS, INC.

Published in the United States of America
by Rowman & Littlefield Publishers, Inc.
4720 Boston Way, Lanham, Maryland 20706

3 Henrietta Street
London WC2E 8LU, England

British Cataloging in Publication Information Available

Library of Congress Cataloging-in-Publication Data

Whitman, Jeffrey P.
The power and value of philosophical skepticism / by Jeffrey P. Whitman.
p. cm.
Includes bibliographical references and index.
1. Skepticism. 2. Knowledge, Theory of. I. Title.
BD201.W54   1996   149'.73—dc20   96–12527   CIP

ISBN 0–8476–8232–3 (cloth : alk. paper)
ISBN 0–8476–8233–1 (pbk. : alk. paper)

Printed in the United States of America

☉™ The paper used in this publication meets the minimum requirements of
American National Standard for Information Sciences—Permanence of
Paper for Printed Library Materials, ANSI Z39.48–1984.

For Laura and Kevin

My Two Favorite Skeptics

Contents

Preface

The idea to write this book came from my studies in areas of philosophy other than epistemology. While examining and teaching various issues in ethics and meta-ethics, I became increasingly convinced that questions of epistemology, questions concerning the nature and extent of our knowledge, needed to be answered before any satisfactory account of our ethical reasoning could be adequately addressed. Thus, I became convinced, along with Descartes, that epistemology was indeed "First Philosophy."

Any examination of epistemology must start by addressing the arguments of skepticism, so that is my focus here. In epistemology, skepticism is the foil against which all theories of knowledge react, and we can learn a great deal by examining these various reactions. Not only do we learn much about these various theories of knowledge, but also, and perhaps more importantly, we learn much about our own nature and the world we inhabit. And that, in the end, is the real purpose of my discussion in this book. How various philosophers and their theories react to skeptical arguments is only part of what an examination of skepticism can teach us. The real lesson I have learned, and one I hope to pass on to readers, is how we, as individuals, ought to react to philosophical skepticism. What should our stance be, as individuals, to philosophical skepticism? If I can at least point out a direction we can follow in answering this question, I will consider my arguments here to have been a success.

Successful or not, I have many people to thank for their considerable help in making this book possible. In particular, I would like to thank Ernest Sosa and James Van Cleve, the two Brown University professors who first excited my interest in epistemology. To Tony Hartle and Peter Stromberg, I owe thanks for giving me the time away from the normal teaching load and other duties at the

United States Military Academy to complete this book. For his many kind and helpful comments on a draft of this work, I thank Louis Pojman and the other anonymous reviewers at Littlefield Adams Books. In addition, I am grateful to Nancy Normann for her patient and detailed desktop publishing. Without her help my work would have contained many more errors and shortcomings. However, any errors or shortcomings that may remain in this work are mine and mine alone. Finally, I owe my deepest gratitude to my wife and two children for putting up with the long hours away from them as I wrote this book. Their good humor and understanding saw me through to the end.

Chapter One

The Problem of Empirical Knowledge

> It may, therefore, be a subject worthy of curiosity, to enquire what is the nature of that evidence, which assures us of any real existence and matter of fact, beyond the present testimony of our senses, or the records of our memory.[1]

In considering Hume's "subject worthy of curiosity," I am, of course, addressing the philosophical problem of empirical knowledge—the knowledge we derive from experience. When we claim to know something about the world around us, what is the justification upon which that claim is based? Given that our senses can deceive us and that our memories are prone to error, what is the status of our putative knowledge of the world around us? Is the skeptic correct in asserting that we really have no knowledge of the external world, our inquiries concerning the nature of the external world forever "incapable of demonstration?"[2] As I hope to show, given certain very plausible assumptions about the nature of empirical knowledge, it does seem as though the skeptic is correct. Claims that we generally take to be unproblematic—Descartes' belief that he is sitting before a fire with a piece of paper in his hand—are seen to rest on a less than solid structure of justification. If this is so, then much, or perhaps even all, of our knowledge concerning the world around us can be called into question.

This issue of skepticism about the external world is a venerable and long-lived one. Plato addresses it in *The Republic* and the *Theaetetus*, Descartes gave the issue new life in his *Meditations on First Philosophy*, and much of the recent work in epistemology is still dedicated to finding some resolution to this problem. Despite this long history of inquiry, however, the problem refuses to go away. When face to face with the skeptical argument, we, like Descartes, often feel "as if [we] had suddenly fallen into a deep whirlpool," and "can neither touch [our feet] to the bottom, nor swim up to the top."[3] In considering how we might address the skeptic and his demands, we often get to a point where, like Wittgenstein, there seems to be little more we can say, and "one would just like to emit an inarticulate sound."[4] The skeptical problem is indeed a difficult one, and as I hope to show, not easily resolved or dismissed.

However, while skepticism about our knowledge of the external world presents philosophers with a fascinating and formidable problem, it presents most of us with no serious impediments to our routine of daily life. As soon as we turn our attention away from the skeptic and his doubts, we find ourselves out of the whirlpool and on terra firma. So why ought we concern ourselves with the skeptic at all? What threat, real or imagined, does epistemic skepticism pose to us? Even if the skeptic is correct (a dubious claim at best), we cannot help but believe we have adequate justification for most of our knowledge concerning the external world.

However, this attitude is far too complacent. We ought not dismiss the skeptic out of hand. The intellectual and ethical consequences are too costly. For if the skeptic is correct about our epistemic predicament regarding empirical knowledge, the relevance of much, if not all, of our everyday moral discourse is threatened. As noted by Hume:

> The experienced train of events is the great *standard* by which all regulate our conduct. Nothing else can be appealed to in the field or in the senate. Nothing else ought ever to be heard of in the school, or in the closet."[5] (Emphasis added.)

If Hume and the skeptic are correct, our judgments concerning right and wrong, good and bad, and the moral requirements for living a virtuous life, seem to be hopeless. Judgments depend upon standards. But if the standards we derive from experience are dubious at best, where does that leave our judgments? And even if, contrary to Hume, our moral standards can be known *a priori* (without appeal to experience), correctly applying these principles in our lives does depend upon some knowledge and understanding of the external world. Without this knowledge, what becomes of the moral guideposts that will direct us in our dealings with the rest of society?[6]

For this reason (and there are others I will raise in the course of this book) the doubts raised by the skeptic deserve our careful consideration. I raise the moral issues first (and no doubt overstate them a bit), because much of my motivation for addressing skepticism derives from these moral considerations. With this in mind, perhaps the rest of my arguments will be more easily understood, and I hope, more convincing.

In addressing skepticism and the problem of the external world, I intend to follow this general course. In the next chapter I will sketch out and argue for an analysis of knowledge based on certain plausible considerations—considerations which I believe are at least prima facie acceptable. The skeptic's arguments will be the subject of chapter 3. In chapters 4, 5, and 6 I will demonstrate how most epistemologists, and the more traditional theories of knowledge, simply ignore crucial issues or engage in question-begging arguments when addressing skepticism. In chapters 7 and 8 I will address the post-analytic solutions to skepticism, focusing on Donald Davidson's and Richard Rorty's contribution to that solution. I will argue for the thesis that the solution they propose has worse consequences than the consequences of the skeptical position which they claim to have dissolved. My own view is that skepticism does not push us to the extremes which Davidson and Rorty advocate. Finally, in the last chapter, I will make my case for how we can live with skepticism and its importance for all philosophical inquiry.

I am especially concerned that the value of philosophical skepticism is generally overlooked or improperly minimized by many of the theories of knowledge I will examine. It is my opinion that only through a careful and full consideration of the skeptical argument can we even begin philosophical inquiry. After all, it was through a recollection and consideration of Hume's skeptical arguments that Kant's "dogmatic slumber" was interrupted.[7] John Dewey also recognized the important link between skepticism and philosophical inquiry:

> That inquiry is related to doubt will, I suppose, be admitted. . . . The admission carries with it an implication regarding the end of inquiry. If inquiry begins in doubt, it terminates in the institution of conditions which remove need for doubt. The latter state of affairs may be designated by the words *belief* and *knowledge*.[8]

I will argue, as Dewey goes on to argue, that instituting the conditions which remove need for doubt is a formidable, if not impossible, task. Therefore, we rarely have the right to terminate inquiry. In other words, there is very little we *really* do know about the external world. In the final analysis then, the important question is not how do we defeat skepticism, but rather how should we react to the apparent triumph of skepticism.

Notes

1. David Hume, *An Enquiry Concerning Human Understanding*, ed. Eric Steinberg (Indianapolis: Hackett Publishing Co., 1977), section IV, 16.
2. Hume, *An Enquiry Concerning Human Understanding*, section XII, 113.
3. Rene Descartes, *Meditations on First Philosophy*, trans. Donald Cress (Indianapolis: Hackett Publishing Co., 1979) (19), 17.
4. Ludwig Wittgenstein, *Philosophical Investigations*, trans. G. E. M. Anscombe,

3rd ed. (New York: Macmillan Publishing Co., 1958), 261.

5. Hume, *An Enquiry Concerning Human Understanding,* section XI, 97–98.

6. I am assuming that our moral discourse is generally of a teleological and not a deontological nature (i.e., it does not solely involve discourse about necessary, *a priori* moral truths), nor is it discourse which merely expresses sentiments or other such psychological attitudes. I will not defend that assumption here except to note that if there are necessary, *a priori* moral truths, few people are in agreement as to what they are. And even if there are such moral truths, knowing when and how to apply the principles they embody requires some knowledge of the external world.

7. Immanuel Kant, *Prolegomena to Any Future Metaphysics*, trans. Lewis White Beck (Indianapolis: Bobbs-Merrill, 1950), 8.

8. John Dewey, *Logic, The Theory of Inquiry* (New York: Holt & Co., 1938), 7.

Chapter Two

An Analysis of Empirical Knowledge

My focus in this book is skepticism, in particular, skepticism and the problem of the external world. However, before we can examine skepticism with regard to our knowledge of the external world, we must reach a clear understanding of the concept of knowledge, in particular empirical knowledge, and what constitutes the external world. In other words, in order to doubt something (in this case, our knowledge of the external world), we must first understand the object of that doubt (the external world and our claim to know something about that world).

The External World

Roughly formulated, when I speak of the external world I am referring to the world around us, or what we may generally think of as our natural environment (e.g., rocks, trees, buildings, other people, etc.). Somewhat more specifically, the external world is all the stuff of the universe which is external to us. This, of course, is still much too vague. What constitutes the *me* to which the world is external? Does it include my body? If it does and I am nothing more than a physical body (the materialist/physicalist view), does it make any sense to talk of a *me* which is not a part of the external world? There would appear to be no *external* world to deal with, and hence, no problem of the external world. Or if there is some *me* which is separate and distinct from the rest of the world, is this *me* entity other than a physical body? And if it is some nonphysical entity (a mental or spiritual entity?), how exactly do I (a nonphysical entity) interact with and come to know the external world (a physical entity)? Does the view that *I* am, in essence, a nonphysical entity automatically make the gap between *me* and the external world too wide to be bridged? If this is the case, we may have defined the problem of the external world in such a way as to beg the question in favor of the skeptic.

As can be seen, answers to these questions, which essentially are metaphysical questions concerning personal identity, tend to force one into a position regarding the problem of the external world. However, I am not interested in questions of personal identity here, and to adequately address this issue now would lead me too far afield. Furthermore, it is my opinion, which I will assert without argumentation for the present, that the problem of the external world is a more fundamental or basic question than the question of personal identity. To allow the problem of personal identity to lead the way in resolving the problem of the external world is to put the cart before the horse. For these reasons I will return to my rough formulation of what I will mean when I refer to the external world.

The external world is the world around us, our natural environment, the stuff of the universe. In it we find (or take ourselves to find) such things as rocks, trees, flowers, buildings, dogs, cats, and so on. It is that part of the world which is not a part of me. It includes other people, as well as my own body.

The skeptic's claim is that we have no real knowledge of the external world. When we claim to *know* that the world is composed of rocks, trees, other people, etc., we are too bold. It is not that the external world does not exist, although some skeptics go on to make this inference.[1] It is merely that our putative knowledge of this world does not meet the standards of real knowledge. But perhaps the skeptic's conception of knowledge differs from our usual conception of this term. Maybe the skeptic is defining knowledge in a peculiar and overly stringent manner. If this is the case, the skeptic's argument may be easily defeated by pointing out the peculiar nature of his definition.

Knowledge Defined

So how ought we to define knowledge? Exactly what do we mean when we or someone else claims to *know* something? The phrase we are interested in clarifying is:

> *S knows that p*, where *S* is the subject of our knowledge claim, and *p* is some claim about the external world.

Let's begin by examining our ordinary conception of the term *know*, as it is used in the above phrase.

There are many uses of the word *know*. I *know* my way around New York City. Larry Bird *knows* basketball. My wife *knows* about physical therapy. These uses of *know* are not the uses of *know* we are interested in. These uses of *know* generally have as their object "how to" kinds of knowledge. I *know how to* get around New York City. Larry Bird *knows how to* play basketball (in this case the term *know* probably indicates a certain degree of competence at playing basketball). My wife, as a physical therapist, *knows how to* give physical therapy to people. The uses of know that we are interested in, however, concern more theoretical knowledge.

John knows that the U.S. Military Academy is located at West Point, New York. Sue knows that William Shakespeare is the author of *Hamlet*. I know that there are two trees in my front yard. Everyone reading this knows that the sum of 1 and 1 is 2. These uses of *know* are more like what interest us. They can be reformulated as claims regarding the truth. John knows that it is *true* that the U.S. Military Academy is located at West Point. We all know that it is *true* that the sum of 1 and 1 is 2. Sue knows that it is *true* that William Shakespeare is the author of *Hamlet*. I know that it is *true* that there are two trees in my front yard. These kinds of knowledge claims, claims that have as their object *truth*, are the kinds of claims which interest us when examining the skeptic's position. This then gives us our first two conditions for knowledge. To know something is to make a *claim* about the *truth*. It is to *believe* that a claim has the property of being *true*.

However, knowledge requires more than merely true belief. If my belief of some claim, e.g., that my wife will be wearing a red sweater when I meet her for lunch, is based merely on a guess, and it turns out that she *is* wearing a red sweater when I meet her for lunch (my belief is therefore true), we would not say that I *knew* before I met her for lunch that she would be wearing a red sweater. My alleged knowledge was based on merely a lucky guess. There would seem to be a difference between knowledge and merely true belief. Plato recognizes this difference when he has Socrates lead Theaetetus to conclude "that true opinion, combined with reason, was knowledge, but that opinion which had no reason was out of the sphere of knowledge."[2]

The difference involves our reasons or justification for believing that a claim is true. If we have good reasons, not merely hunches or lucky guesses, which justify our belief that a claim is true, and it turns out that the claim is true, then we can be said to have knowledge. This then is the third condition for knowledge: good reasons or *justification*.

We are now in a position to more clearly flesh out our analysis of knowledge.

S knows that p, where *S* is the subject of our knowledge claim, and *p* is some claim about the external world, if and only if:

(a) *S* believes that *p*,

(b) *p* is true, and

(c) *S* is justified in believing that *p*.

There is, however, one more qualification or condition to be added to our analysis. As Edmund Gettier has pointed out, we may satisfy the three conditions above and yet not have knowledge that *p* if our justification was based on a false assumption.[3] Suppose I believe that I have a pen in a certain notebook on my desk. I am justified in having this belief because I always keep a pen in that notebook and never remove it except to write in that notebook. After I finish using it I always return it to the notebook so I can be assured of always having something to write with when I take this notebook with me. I *know* there is a pen in that notebook. However, suppose one day, while I am away from my desk, a friend borrows this pen. I no longer *know* there is a pen in my notebook because my belief that there is a pen there is no longer true. However, suppose on that same day my wife buys me a new pen and places it in that notebook as a surprise gift. Now my belief that there is a pen in my notebook is true, but it is essentially based on a false assumption that no one removed the pen from the notebook. Therefore it seems that we cannot say that I *know* there is a pen in my notebook.

How might our analysis of knowledge be saved from this and other kinds of Gettier-type counterexamples? Unfortunately, there is no quick fix available, no simple fourth condition, that can be added to the three conditions already enumerated. Philosophers have advanced numerous proposals, but all have been found lacking in one way or another. Initially many thought that the Gettier problem (as these counterexamples came to be known) could be solved by adding the fourth condition that our justification cannot be essentially based on false beliefs. However, in a now famous example from Carl Ginet, this no false belief condition was shown to be inadequate.

Henry is driving through the countryside and he *correctly* identifies a red barn in the distance. However, unknown to Henry, a number of red barn facades (indistinguishable at a distance from real red barns) have been placed throughout the area he is now driving through. We would not want to say that Henry knows he is seeing a red barn, but his failure to know is not based on any false belief. Thus he could fulfill all our conditions for knowledge, including this new, no false belief condition and still not know he sees a red barn in the distance.[4]

Much has been written and continues to be written concerning the Gettier problem.[5] Therefore, given the many different solutions that have been proposed and debated, I will not, for the present, settle on one view and defend it. Instead I propose the following fourth condition as a way of recognizing that our analysis of knowledge is not yet complete. To recapitulate:

> *S knows that p*, where *S* is the subject of our knowledge claim, and *p* is some claim about the external world, if and only if:
> (a) *S* believes that *p*,
> (b) *p* is true,

(c) S is justified in believing that p, and
(d) S's justification is not subject to Gettier-type counterexamples.

This analysis of knowledge, while a bit more precise than our everyday, nonreflective understanding of knowledge, does not seem unusual or peculiar. Nor does it seem, Gettier problem aside, an overly strenuous standard for knowledge. The conditions are reasonable and generally accepted by most philosophers. We surely would not want to accuse the skeptic who is using this analysis of employing a special or idiosyncratic definition of knowledge. For the time being at least then, we can lay aside this concern. There is, however, some clarification that must yet occur before we can get to the skeptic's arguments.

Justification and Metajustification

The first item we need to clarify concerns justification. Since the time of Plato, much of the work of epistemology has centered on this concept of justification as it applies to knowledge (epistemic justification). For Plato it was justification which "tied down" correct opinion and made it knowledge.[6] Others characterize epistemic justification as having adequate evidence for p[7] or having the right to be sure that p is true.[8] But what counts as having adequate evidence and what gives us the right to be sure? When is our justification adequate to support our claim to *know* that p?

As a start we might say that our justification is adequate when it is aimed at acquiring true beliefs. This is the hallmark of epistemic justification. It provides us with the standards for judging our beliefs as either true or false. If we meet these standards when formulating our beliefs, we have done our intellectual duty as cognitive, rational beings. This is not to say that other forms of justification are not important when we are forming beliefs. However, these other kinds of justification, in that they don't have true belief as their goal, don't count as epistemic justification.

For example, Pascal's wager for justifying the belief that God exists is an example of nonepistemic justification. Belief in the existence of God is justified, not because this belief is true, but because it is the safest bet. Such a justification is prudential rather than epistemic in nature. It is aimed at safeguarding the believer's future after death rather than at attaining true belief. Another example might involve belief in the fidelity of one's spouse. You may not *know* that your spouse has remained faithful (you have never bothered to conduct an investigation into this aspect of your married life), but based on your many years of marriage and the relationship you both share, you are certainly justified in your belief that your spouse has been faithful—even, perhaps, if you were presented with a certain amount of information indicating otherwise. Again, your justification is not aimed at discovering the truth but is rather a kind of moral justification based on the relationship of marriage. However, if we are to fulfill our intellectual duty in forming our beliefs, it is epistemic justification, and not these other kinds of justification, which will interest us.

The second part of the answer to this question of epistemic justification is related to the first. If epistemic justification is to provide us with the standards for ascertaining the truth of our beliefs, how are we to know that these standards are, in fact, adequately truth-conducive? Why should we adopt these particular standards of epistemic justification and not some others? As Chisholm remarks, "we hope . . . that our marks of evidence will also be marks of truth."[9] But in order to move beyond mere hope and adequately address this issue, we seem to need another level of justification—what Laurence BonJour calls a *metajustification*. This metajustification would function as "a *vindication* of the proposed standards of epistemic justification."[10]

As BonJour points out, there are two main difficulties inherent in providing a metajustification. They both concern the materials one may use in constructing such an argument. As our interest is focused on empirical knowledge, empirical premises in our metajustificatory argument must be ruled out as question begging. For if we were to use empirical premises in constructing our argument for a standard of epistemic justification, that empirical premise will stand in need of justification. If we justify it by appeal to our own standard of justification (which in turn is justified in part by this very same premise), our justification is obviously circular. If we justify it by appeal to some other standard, we have abandoned the claim that the epistemic standard we are arguing for is the correct one. Thus it would seem that our metajustificatory argument will have to be an *a priori* argument, and "it is certainly far from obvious how such an *a priori* argument might go."[11]

Secondly, the materials used in our metajustification must be available to our putative knower. If our metajustificatory argument is not reasonably within the grasp of the putative knower, there seems to be little sense in which she can claim to know something is true based on this argument. There is much more to be said on this point, but I will defer my arguments until my discussion of externalism and internalism.

Now if providing a metajustification is such a difficult undertaking, what is the reward. Put simply, the reward is truth. Metajustification is what bridges the gap between justification and truth. Only if our standards of epistemic justification can be shown to lead to true belief, i.e., the standards are appropriately truth-conducive, can the skeptic's concerns (how do we know the truth concerning the external world) be fully and adequately addressed. This leads directly to our final preliminary issue: truth.

Truth

"To say of what is that it is not, or of what is not that it is, is false, while to say of what is that it is, and of what is not that it is not, is true."[12] While Aristotle's definition of truth may be overly simplistic and may initially strike one as vacuous, it does seem to capture at least one important characteristic of truth, that truth is a relational concept. There is the carrier or vehicle of truth (or falsehood), and there is the reality to which this carrier corresponds (or fails to correspond). The vehicle of truth is what I have been generally been referring to as a *claim*. Other terms which might be seen as synonymous with claim include judgment, declarative sentence or statement, belief, or proposition. I have purposely avoided the term *proposition* up to this point because of the controversy which surrounds the technical use of that term in philosophy. In particular I wished to avoid questions concerning the ontological status of propositions and a discussion of what truly constitutes a proposition. However, these issues do not appear to have any significant bearing on my arguments. If we understand the term *proposition* as it is most normally understood—the abstract entity or idea which we generally expressed in a simple declarative sentence—the proposition will be our vehicle or carrier of truth. The truth or falsity of our claims, beliefs, statements, etc., will be determined by the truth or falsity of the propositions they express.

The reality to which our propositions correspond is the world as it really is. This is what constitutes Kant's world of the thing-in-itself. It is the objective, external world, not dependent on human thought or perception for its existence. This is the view that Hilary Putnam refers to as *metaphysical realism*. "On this perspective [metaphysical realism], the world consists of some fixed totality of mind-independent objects. There is exactly one true and complete description of 'the way the world is.'"[13] It is this description which constitute the facts to which our propositions correspond. Thus, to return to Aristotle's definition, a proposition is true when it expresses what *is* in the mind-independent, real world. The proposition that there are two trees in my front yard is true if and only if there *really are* two trees in my front yard. Truth is this correspondence between our propositions and the objective reality of the real world.

Of course this is just one—the correspondence theory—of the many stories which can be told in explicating truth. Another is the coherence theory of truth, often associated with some form of idealism (the view that the external world is created by the mind), which asserts that truth is a matter of coherence within a system of beliefs. The system of beliefs is real, but there is no thing-in-itself world to which these beliefs correspond. Yet another theory asserts that our ability to verify a statement is what makes it true or false. This theory had its origins with Moritz Schlick and the Vienna Circle, and is well explicated in A. J. Ayer's *Language, Truth, and Logic*. However, in that it is largely a linguistic treatment of what I view as an essentially metaphysical issue, it seems in the end to leave the question of truth unresolved. Then there are also theories which simply deny the truth of metaphysical realism. The view here is that there is no mind-independent, external world which we can describe in any meaningful way, therefore to speak of such a world is futile nonsense.[14] Such antirealist theories appear to reject truth in favor of mere justification and again may merely be a linguistic solution to a metaphysical problem.

At any rate, these various other theories of truth have largely been developed to deal with the problem of epistemic skepticism and seem to have no presumption in their favor. I will, however, deal with each of them more fully as I address the various solutions to skepticism. For the present, I will presume that the correspondence theory of truth is the correct one. It certainly seems the most plausible to me in that it most clearly agrees with our common sense view of truth. Also, the skeptic's argument is most compelling within the context of metaphysical realism and a correspondence theory of truth. As my purpose is to closely examine skepticism as it applies to our knowledge of the external world, it only seems prudent to start with the most plausible and natural understanding of the *external world* and *truth*. Under the pressures of the skeptic's argument, we may find reason to change this initial presumption—but not until then.

A Summary of My Analysis

I am now in a position to summarize the results of my analysis of empirical knowledge up to this point. I began with a definition of empirical knowledge.

> *S knows that p*, where *S* is the subject of our knowledge claim, and *p* is some claim about the external world, if and only if:
> (a) *S* believes that *p*,
> (b) *p* is true,
> (c) *S* is justified in believing that *p*, and
> (d) *S*'s justification is not subject to Gettier-type counterexamples.

I further elaborated on some of the terms of this definition. The external world was analyzed within the context of *metaphysical realism*. Truth was analyzed within the context of a *correspondence theory of truth*. And justification was analyzed within the context of a twofold requirement consisting of *epistemic justification* and *metajustification*. The results are summarized below.

> (A) Metaphysical Realism—There exists an objective, mind-independent, external world.
> (B) Correspondence Theory of Truth—True belief consists of a relation of correspondence between propositions (as expressed by our beliefs, judgments, claims, etc.) and how the world really is.
> (C) Epistemic Justification and Metajustification—A belief is epistemically justified if and only if the standards used by the putative knower to justify the belief are aimed at acquiring the truth and these standards are themselves justified by the putative knower as being adequately truth-conducive.

The skeptical argument I will examine seeks to deny that our claims to know something about the external world adequately meets the standards for knowledge I have thus far laid out. The skeptic is not making a metaphysical claim about the existence of the external world or truth, although his arguments may depend upon certain metaphysical claims. He is merely making an epistemic claim about our knowledge of the external world, namely, that it fails to meet the standards for real knowledge. With my preliminary analysis of empirical knowledge completed, it is now time to turn to the skeptic's argument. His argument seems to me to be a good one and not easily refuted.

Notes

1. Kant, concerned with addressing this problem of the existence of the external world, considered the lack of a proof for its existence "the scandal of philosophy."

2. Plato, *Theaetetus*, trans. Benjamin Jowett (Indianapolis: Bobbs-Merrill/Library of Liberal Arts, 1949) (201), 72.

3. Edmund Gettier, "Is Justified True Belief Knowledge?" in *Knowing: Essays in the Theory of Knowledge*, ed. Michael Roth and Leon Galis, 2nd ed. (Lanham, Md.: University Press of America, 1984), 35–38.

4. For more on this example see Alvin Goldman, "Discrimination and Perceptual Knowledge," *The Journal of Philosophy* 73.20 (1976): 771–91.

5. See George Pappas, ed., *Justification and Knowledge* (Dordrecht, Holland: D. Reidel Publishing Co., 1979), and Michael Roth and Leon Galis, eds., *Knowing: Essays in the Theory of Knowledge* for some of what has been written on the Gettier problem.

6. Plato, *Meno* in *Five Dialogues*, trans. G. M. A. Grube (Indianapolis: Hackett Publishing Co., 1981) (98), 86.

7. Roderick Chisholm, *Perceiving: A Philosophical Study* (Ithaca, N.Y.: Cornell University Press, 1957), 16.

8. Alfred J. Ayer, *The Problem of Knowledge* (New York: Penguin, 1956), 35.

9. Chisholm, *Perceiving*, 38.

10. Laurence BonJour, *The Structure of Empirical Knowledge* (Cambridge: Harvard University Press, 1985), 9.

11. BonJour, *The Structure of Empirical Knowledge*, 10.

12. Aristotle, *Metaphysics*. In *The Complete Works of Aristotle*. Ed. Jonathan Barnes. Princeton: Princeton University Press, 1984, (1011b25), 1597.

13. Hilary Putnam, *Reason, Truth, and History* (Cambridge: Cambridge University Press, 1981), 49.

14. Richard Rorty's pragmatic idea of truth is who I principally have in mind here. I will have much more to say on this point in later chapters.

Chapter Three

Skepticism

[The skeptic] states what appears to himself and announces his own impression in an undogmatic way, without making any positive assertion regarding the external realities.[1]

Sextus Empiricus' remarks come from one of the earliest formulations of a theory of skepticism. While Pyrrho of Elis (c. 365–275 B.C.) was really the first philosopher to develop skepticism in a systematic way, he himself wrote nothing. Sextus Empiricus, a skeptical philosopher of the 2nd century A.D., most completely captures Pyrrho's views in his three-volume work, *Outlines of Pyrrhonism*.[2] I begin this chapter with Sextus Empiricus because I want to first focus on a certain attitude (an attitude with which Sextus begins his *Outlines*) that seems inherent in all forms of skepticism, and for that matter, in all good philosophy. The attitude is one of antidogmatism with respect to our beliefs, whether they be our moral beliefs, our metaphysical beliefs, or our epistemic beliefs.

In our everyday life we accept the common sense assumption that our sense perceptions give us unproblematic knowledge of the external world. If I see two trees in my front yard I ought to believe that there are two trees in my front yard. Furthermore, that belief is true. In fact, it is self-evident that there are two trees in my front yard. There is no need to examine critically the deliverances of my senses in order to determine that there are two trees in my front yard. The assumption is that our sense perceptions match the things-in-themselves (i.e., match the way the world really is). In general, we uncritically accept this common sense assumption as we make our way in the world. It is a sort of dogma born of, what many might label, a practical necessity.

The skeptic does not dogmatically accept this common sense assumption. However, he is not alone in rejecting this sort of dogmatism. Most philosophers working in the field of epistemology reject this assumption as well. They, like the skeptic, endeavor to critically examine the assumptions of common sense. However, while it is not an attitude unique to skepticism, it is especially important in understanding and appreciating skeptical thought. It is one of the first pillars of skepticism—a rejection of dogmatic assumption in favor of critical reflection and examination—and it is an attitude I will often return to.

The difference between most epistemologists and the skeptic is in the conclusions they draw from their critical reflections. The epistemologist generally finds a way to save our knowledge of the external world. She will either repair the common sense model which forms the basis for this assumption or offer a better model as a theory of knowledge. The skeptic, on the other hand, argues that a critical examination of this assumption reveals its dubious nature. The connection between our sense perceptions and the external world is seen as problematic in the extreme, to the point that it threatens all our knowledge of the external world. How is it that the skeptic reaches this conclusion, a conclusion which seems so divorced from our common sense view of the world? This skepticism with regard to our sense perceptions begins with the apparent dichotomy between what we perceive and the world as it really is, between appearances and reality.

Appearances and Reality

Returning to Sextus Empiricus, we find skepticism defined as:

> a mental attitude, which opposes appearances to judgement in any way whatsoever with the result that . . . we are brought firstly to a state of mental suspense and next to a state of "unperturbedness" or quietude.[3]

The view seems to be that we should confine ourselves to appearances, or what Sextus also calls "phenomena," and not make any judgments concerning the nature of the objective, things-in-themselves world from these phenomena. Instead we are urged to suspend judgment and in this way escape the insoluble complexities of life and attain a state of "unperturbedness." While I am not so sure that this "state of mental suspense" will have the salubrious effect predicted by Pyrrho and Sextus, that is not my focus here. What I mean to emphasize is the distinction between appearances, or what we might generally label perceptual beliefs, and judgments concerning reality.

Plato presents us with one of the first arguments employing the appearance/reality distinction. While engaged in a refutation of Protagoras' thesis that "man is the measure of all things," Plato makes the point that appearances do vary from one observer to another.[4] For example, while a man may appear tall when viewed close up, this same man will appear short from a distance. Or to borrow an example from Bertrand Russell, the shape of a table, which is *really* rectangular, will vary as we change our perspective.[5] When viewed from almost any angle, except maybe from directly above the table, the opposite sides will not appear parallel, and the angles of the corners will not be perpendicular. But if the shape changes as our perspective changes, how do we know the *real* shape of the table? Which perspective is the *correct* one?

Not only do appearances differ from what we consider reality, but we can also point to examples where we are deceived by our perceptions. A coat which may appear blue under normal, white lighting, will appear green under yellow lighting. Nonetheless, the coat is *really* blue. Similarly, through some clever arrangement of mirrors it may be made to appear to me that there is an apple on my desk, when in *actuality* the apple is on a chair in the hallway. While waiting in a car at a traffic light, the car beside me may appear to move forward, when in *reality* my car is drifting backwards.

I have italicized words like *real*, *really*, and *actuality*, because when we are dealing with perceptual beliefs it seems very difficult to make a judgment concerning what is *real* or *actual*. And this is exactly the point the skeptic wants to make. When we claim to know something based on our perceptual beliefs or appearances, we are assuming the common sense view that having a perceptual belief entails that the belief in question is true, i.e., it reflects reality, the thing-in-itself world of Kant. Yet, as these examples indicate, such an entailment between perception and reality does not hold.

There are other examples that have been used to question this entailment between perception and reality. The possibility of hallucinations, as a result of fatigue, fear, euphoria, use of hallucinogenic drugs, to include alcohol, argue against our common sense belief in this entailment. Descartes' formulates the hypothesis that all our perceptions are the result of a dream. Seated before a fire in his dressing gown with a piece of paper in his hand, he asks himself how can he be sure he is not dreaming that he is seated before a fire in his dressing gown with a piece of paper in his hand.[6] Unless he can rule out the possibility that he is dreaming, it doesn't seem he knows anything about the world around him, including whether or not he really is seated before a fire in his dressing gown with a piece of paper in his hand. Descartes also postulates the existence of an evil genius who works to constantly deceive us.

> Thus I will suppose not a supremely good God, the source of truth, but rather an evil genius, as clever and deceitful as he is powerful, who has directed his entire effort to mislead me. I will regard the heavens, the air, the earth, colors,

shapes, sounds, and all external things as but the deceptive games of my dreams, with which he lays snares for my credulity.[7]

Hilary Putnam updates Descartes' evil genius with his "brain in a vat" example.[8] He asks you to imagine that an evil scientist has removed your brain from your body and placed it in a vat of nutrients which keeps the brain alive. The brain is then hooked up to a sophisticated computer which gives you the illusion that everything is normal. Your perceptions remain the same as they were before this operation—you see and feel objects, other people, etc.—but these perceptions are the result of inputs from the computer and have no connection with the real world. All your perceptions are mere illusion.

Now although Putnam, Descartes and others go on to show how these examples are either somehow flawed or don't lead to the kind of skepticism they seem to entail, in the end I find their arguments wanting (as I hope to show in the next two chapters). What I mainly intend to do now, is to get the skeptic's argument out in the open. The basic form of the argument is something like this:

(1) It is always logically possible that the experiences of a person having a true perceptual belief and the experiences of a person having a false perceptual belief are indistinguishable (as the above examples are meant to show).

(2) If it is always logically possible that the experiences of a person having a true perceptual belief and the experiences of a person having a false perceptual belief are indistinguishable, then we can never know whether any of our perceptual beliefs are true or false.

Conclusion:

(3) We can never know whether any of our perceptual beliefs are true or false.

As will be seen in future chapters, this skeptical argument is attacked on many fronts by many different theories of knowledge. In my view, however, this argument, combined with my definition of knowledge from the last chapter, can be refuted only at great cost—a cost I will argue is unacceptable. But before we get to that, I would like to look again, in some greater depth, at a critical piece of the skeptical position. What I refer to is the thesis of metaphysical realism, i.e., that there is a real world which is the object of our knowledge. Without a real world, distinguishing between reality and appearance—a dichotomy which seems crucial to the skeptic's position—is not possible. While I made a presumptive case for metaphysical realism in the last chapter, I want to strengthen that presumption before moving on.

The Real World and Its Alternatives

I begin my defense of the real world and metaphysical realism by making a distinction, lest there be some confusion. Metaphysical realism, to recall, is the thesis that there exists an objective, mind-independent, external world. The alternative most often opposed to realism is a kind of Berkeleian idealism. However, this is not the alternative to realism that I find the most worrisome. While Berkeley believes that the material objects of the world are nothing but ideas or objects of thought in our minds, he also believes that they are not "empty appearances," but "real beings."[9] For if the ideas are not in some sense real, it is hard to imagine how we come to have them. They may be in the head, but they are real nonetheless. To push idealism any deeper than this seems incoherent or sets us off on an infinite regress of ideas about ideas. So although Berkeley is not a *metaphysical realist* concerning the material objects of the world, it does seem clear that he is a *realist* in the sense that ideas or objects of thought in our minds are real. Therefore, the alternative I mean to oppose to realism (and argue against) is *not* a kind of Berkeleian idealism.

The view I take exception to is not idealism but antirealism. Michael Dummett, in arguing for antirealism, draws the distinction between realism and antirealism as follows:

> Realism I characterize as the belief that statements in the disputed class [e.g., statements about the physical world, mental events, mathematical statements] possess an objective truth-value, independent of our means of knowing it: they are true or false in virtue of a reality existing independently of us. The anti-realist opposes to this the view that statements of the disputed class are to be understood only by reference to the sort of thing which we count as evidence for that class.[10]

Dummett's antirealism is not really a metaphysical theory—it makes no claim about what exists in the world—but a linguistic theory about meaning, as he makes clear in a later passage.

> For [the antirealist] the meaning of a statement is intrinsically connected with that which we count as evidence for or against the statement; and there is nothing to prevent a statement's being so used that we do not treat anything as conclusively verifying it [my emphasis].[11]

However, there seems to be an implicit metaphysical claim in Dummett's view, and it is this claim that I find especially troubling. The Berkeleian idealist at least acknowledges the reality of his ideas. He knows his own head. The antirealist, on the other hand, seems to know nothing (or everything?) because there is nothing to know.

According to Dummett's brand of antirealism, if the ability to verify a statement is what gives that statement meaning, i.e., assigns the statement a truth-value, any statement which cannot be verified is meaningless. Verification and truth are seen as one and the same. But isn't verification just a type of epistemic justification? And if justification and truth are conflated in this way, what work is truth accomplishing in the theory? The obvious answer is none at all. To verify (justify) one's belief in p is to know p. There is no need to even mention truth as a criterion for knowledge. Furthermore, even the possibility of an independent reality is ruled out. As BonJour makes clear in his discussion of truth, antirealism "amounts to a denial that we are able to say (or even think?) anything which purports to describe independent . . . reality."[12]

Richard Rorty, recognizing this implication of antirealism, scraps truth altogether. In *Philosophy and the Mirror of Nature* he concludes that philosophy's obsession with epistemology, and its goal of discovering the objective truth, ought to be set aside. There is no ahistorical, objective truth to be discovered according to Rorty. Instead of searching for some nonexistent truth we should be engaged in a form of "edifying philosophy" which concentrates on hermeneutics and the "conversation of mankind."[13] While I will have much more to say about Rorty's position and others like it in chapters 7 and 8, let me point out this much here. At the very least Rorty seems to be begging the question posed by the skeptic. It is not that he has solved the problem of skepticism; he has merely asserted that it is *not* a problem. With no truth to discover, we cannot have any doubts about our knowledge of the truth. But this is a radical solution to the skeptical problem, a solution, as I will later argue, that has worse consequences than the problem it purportedly dissolves. Furthermore, it is largely a semantical solution revolving around a theory of meaning that does not really address the skeptic's concerns. The antirealist's theory of meaning (meaning as verification) declares the skeptic's arguments as meaningless. Yet the skeptical problem itself goes beyond mere issues of language and does not disappear through the application of some linguistic sleight-of-hand. In what sense are the skeptic's arguments meaningless? Surely they are not gibberish. We are all able to understand and make sense of them. We can discuss the skeptic's arguments and even be influenced by them. If a theory of meaning asserts that the skeptic's doubts and questions are meaningless, so much the worse for that theory.

Skepticism concerning our knowledge of the external world is not so easily brushed aside as Rorty, Dummett, and other antirealists would have us believe. Before we are pushed to such extreme solutions to skepticism, we need to give skepticism a more charitable hearing. Our intellectual duty demands nothing less. So for the time being, I believe it is plausible to stand by the thesis of metaphysical realism and reject the antirealist alternative. I will have reason to revisit antirealism later on in chapter 7, but not until other, more plausible alternatives are explored.

Satisfying the Skeptic

Before moving on to the next chapters and an examination of various theories of knowledge, it would be helpful to pause here and ask what exactly does the skeptic demand of a successful theory of knowledge. All theories of knowledge seek to answer one of two related questions: (1) What do we know? and (2) How do we know? In the second chapter, where I laid out my analysis of knowledge, I was primarily interested in the latter question. There I was concerned with formulating the criteria for knowledge, the criteria which tell us whether or not we really know something. These criteria tell us *how* knowledge is possible (or not possible). In this chapter I have focused more on the first of these two questions (what do we know) and the skeptic's response—nothing (at least nothing from our perceptions).

Of course to say we know nothing at all is a very radical form of skepticism. A less radical skepticism might grant the possibility of knowledge within certain domains while denying such a possibility in others. The skeptic could even concede that what we take to be knowledge actually is, by and large, genuine knowledge. However, he might go on to assert that none of it is certain knowledge. It can all be called into doubt. Given the various forms skepticism might take, what is the form I intend to use? If we are to understand what it will take to satisfy the skeptic, we need to be clear on the extent of his skepticism.

The skeptical view I mean to examine here is concerned with our knowledge of the external world as given to us by our perceptions. As I hope I made clear earlier, I do not intend to question the existence of the external world but merely our knowledge of it. Also, the skeptical position I intend to champion does not rely on some special or exalted concept of knowledge. In my earlier analysis knowledge. The criteria of knowledge that I began with seems eminently plausible and in keeping with our everyday notions. The skeptic does not need a special sense of *knowledge* to make his point. And what is his point? The skeptic's thesis is really a statement about the human condition.

The skeptic presents us with some logical possibilities—we are dreaming, we are brains in a vat, we are under the influence of hallucinogenic drugs—and uses these possibilities to threaten all of our knowledge of the external world. He goes beyond the fairly innocent claim that all of us as human beings are fallible. It is not merely that we sometimes make mistakes or that we sometimes act irrationally. The claim is more general than that. Even given our best efforts and no mistakes of reasoning, our condition is such that we can never know anything about the external world. For unless we can eliminate the possibility that we are now dreaming or are brains in a vat, it seems wrong to say we know anything about the external world. An example used by Barry Stroud will help make my point.[14]

Stroud asks us to imagine people are being trained as airplane spotters by the military. They are specifically trained to identify two types of airplanes—

Stroud calls them F-planes and E-planes. As their instructors and manuals teach them, F-planes have characteristics x, y, and z, while E-planes have characteristics x, y, and w. Once fully trained, a spotter, upon seeing a plane with characteristics x, y, and z, will report to headquarters that she has spotted an F-plane. If questioned about the spotting and how she knows the plane is an F-plane, the spotter will tell us the plane she spotted has the characteristics (x, y, z) of an F-plane. Assuming it is a good spotting, i.e., conditions are such that the spotter gets a clear look at the plane and is making no mistakes, the spotter is well trained, alert and conscientious, she is justified in claiming to know she has spotted an F-plane. Likewise, if she had only identified characteristics x and y on the plane, she would not be justified (and would not know) she had spotted an F-plane. Until she identifies character z on the plane, it could be an E-plane. If she prematurely claims to have spotted an F-plane, before she identifies characteristic z on the plane, we wouldn't want to attribute knowledge to her in this case. She may get lucky and it may turn out to be an F-plane, but she would not be justified in claiming to know it was an F-plane.

Suppose next, as Stroud does, that there is another type of airplane, a G-plane, that also has characteristics x, y, and z. During training the spotters are not told about these G-planes because it would make the identifying of F-planes extremely difficult. Even when examined on the ground and from fairly close up it is difficult to distinguish an F-plane from a G-plane. Furthermore, we might imagine the G-plane is not generally found in the area our spotters will be working, and it does not constitute much of a military threat anyway. Based on these practical military considerations, the spotters are never told about the G-plane.

However, given this additional information, what do we say about the spotter who claims to have spotted an F-plane based on her knowledge that the airplane she sees has characteristics x, y, and z? The airplane spotter, with her training and knowledge, is certainly justified in claiming to know that the airplane she has observed is an F-plane, but don't we as outside observers know better? Furthermore, if we tell the spotter about the existence of G-planes, we can imagine that her response to this additional information would be to agree with us and admit she does not know that the plane is an F-plane. Just as she did not know the plane was an F-plane when she had only identified characteristics x and y on it, so now she does not know it is an F-plane even though she has identified characteristics x, y, and z on it. The spotter needs more information before she can justifiably identify it as an F-plane, namely, she would have to rule out the possibility of it being a G-plane. It doesn't matter that the spotter has no way to rule out this possibility (she is observing the plane from a distance when even from close up distinguishing the two types of planes is difficult), she would still not claim to know it was an F-plane. With the new information on G-planes she would have to admit that she just doesn't know what kind of plane it is.

Descartes' dream argument operates in exactly the same manner. In order to know he is sitting before a fire with a piece of paper in his hand, he must rule out the possibility that he is dreaming. In order for the airplane spotter to know she has spotted an F-plane, she must rule out the possibility that it is a G-plane. If Descartes is unable to rule out the dream possibility, he cannot claim to know he is sitting before a fire with a piece of paper in his hand—or anything about the world around him. What Stroud's airplane spotter example makes clear is that the skeptic is not making use of some special, extraordinary sense of knowledge. It is only by appeal to our everyday common sense notions of knowledge that Stroud's and Descartes' examples work. In fact, the force and intuitive appeal of skepticism rests on the skeptic's use of our everyday, common sense understanding of knowledge.

But while the argument for skepticism rests on our common sense understanding of knowledge, the conclusion—our perceptions give us no knowledge of the external world—defies common sense. Because the conclusion does such violence to the common sense view of our knowledge, we want to reject skepticism. The skeptic seems to be requiring more of knowledge than we normally demand. If real knowledge is so difficult to attain, if we are all in the predicament that the airplane spotters find themselves in, how is it that in everyday life these skeptical possibilities do not concern us? In our normal day-to-day lives we claim to know all sorts of things about the external world. How does this knowledge differ from the skeptic's conception of knowledge?

The difference, as Stroud clearly points out, concerns a distinction between use and meaning.[15] Our conception of knowledge remains the same regardless of the context. What we *mean* by epistemic terms such as "knowledge" and "know" does not change whether we are speaking philosophically, scientifically, or in everyday life. This is what the airplane spotter example is meant to demonstrate. Our conception of knowledge remains the same in the context of the airplane spotters, as well as in Descartes' dream context. What does change from context to context is our use of these terms.

In our everyday life we are forced to operate under a set of practical constraints. As a result we are forced to make certain assumptions, e.g., there are no G-planes, I am not now dreaming. We are allowed these assumptions because our discourse in this context is not solely aimed at the truth. More often, ease of communication, the need to cooperate, concern with self-preservation—in a word, *expediency*—is the focus of our everyday discourse. These practical constraints impel us to *use* the term differently. This is why the trainers of our airplane spotters did not tell them about G-planes. Within the context of the war effort it would have served no useful purpose. As the goal was to train the spotters to distinguish F-planes from E-planes, to mention the G-plane would only lead to confusion. For all *practical purposes*, a spotter *knows* he has spotted an F-plane if it has characteristics x, y, and z. However, when the trainers are pressed to consider the spotter's knowledge within a more theoretical/philosophical context, they would readily admit that the spotters could not know, solely on the basis of identifying x, y, and z, that they had spotted an F-plane. After all, it could be a G-plane.

Any argument against skepticism which claims the skeptic is trading on a different meaning of knowledge than implied in our everyday usage, fails to recognize the distinction between meaning and use. Depending on the purpose or context of our discourse, our usage of epistemic terms changes. If our primary goal is on practical, everyday concerns, the skeptical possibilities will tend to be set aside in favor of expediency. But if our goal is centered on a general theoretical accounting of human knowledge, which is the context of philosophical discourse, the skeptical possibility cannot so easily be ignored. However, in either context—the everyday practical and the theoretical/philosophical—our conception of knowledge remains the same.

Perhaps now the demands of the skeptic can be brought into tighter focus. It really boils down to two principal requirements. First, the skeptic is interested in the theoretical rather than the practical realm. His argument should be viewed within this context. We cannot dismiss his conclusion merely because it does not accord with our common sense notions as they operate within the practical realm. Second, the skeptic's concept of knowledge is not somehow special or extraordinary. To attribute an extraordinary conception of knowledge to the skeptic is to beg the question against the skeptical position. With these two requirements in mind, it is time to examine a number of theories of knowledge.

Notes

1. Sextus Empiricus, *Outlines of Pyrrhonism* (London: Loeb Classical Library, 1933) (I, 18), 11.
2. Antony Flew, *A Dictionary of Philosophy*, 2nd ed. (New York: St. Martin's Press, 1979), 294 and 326.
3. Sextus, *Outlines of Pyrrhonism* (I, 15), 7.
4. Plato, *Theaetetus,* trans. Benjamin Jowett. (Indianapolis: Bobbs-Merrill/Library of Liberal Arts, 1949) (152–57), 12–19.
5. Bertrand Russell, *The Problems of Philosophy* (Oxford: Oxford University Press, 1959), 10–11.
6. Descartes, *Meditations on First Philosophy* (19), 14.
7. Descartes, *Meditations on First Philosophy* (22), 16.
8. Hilary Putnam, *Reason, Truth, and History* (Cambridge: Cambridge University Press, 1981), 5–6.
9. George Berkeley, *Three Dialogues Between Hylas and Philonous* in *Principles, Dialogues, and Philosophical Correspondence*, ed. Colin Turbayne. (New York: McMillan Publishing Co., 1987) (III, 15), 191.
10. Michael Dummett, "Realism," in *Truth and Other Enigmas* (Cambridge: Harvard University Press, 1978), 146.
11. Dummett, "Realism," 162.
12. BonJour, *The Structure of Empirical Knowledge*, 162.
13. See especially chapters VII and VIII of Richard Rorty's *Philosophy and the*

Mirror of Nature (Princeton: Princeton University Press, 1979).

14. Barry Stroud, *The Significance of Philosophical Scepticism* (New York: Clarendon Press, 1984), 68*ff.* The example originally comes from Thompson Clarke, "The Legacy of Skepticism," in *The Journal of Philosophy* 69 (November 1972): 759*ff.*

15. Stroud, *The Significance of Philosophical Scepticism*, 75.

Chapter Four

Doxastic Theories of Knowledge

In discussing theories of knowledge and how they deal with the skeptical problem, it seems helpful to divide the various theories into several broad categories. Following John Pollock, I will start by classifying theories as either *doxastic* or *nondoxastic*.[1] A doxastic theory focuses on the beliefs the putative knower holds or that knower's *doxastic state*. The assumption here is that everything a person knows about the world can be stated in terms of some first person belief or series of beliefs (e.g., I believe I see an apple on the desk). These beliefs are in turn justified by other beliefs that we hold (e.g., I believe I see something round and red on the desk that appears to be an apple). In other words, epistemic justification for everything one knows about the world depends *entirely* upon what beliefs one holds—the doxastic state of the subject. This seems like a very plausible assumption, and it is one that was not questioned until fairly recently.

A non-doxastic theory of knowledge denies this assumption made by doxastic theories. For these theories, epistemic justification does not depend entirely on the subject's doxastic state. Rather there are considerations other than the putative knower's beliefs which enter into that knower's epistemic justification. What exactly these considerations are and how they are to be made out is sometimes difficult to understand, but I will leave that to the next chapter. This chapter I want to devote to examining doxastic theories, of which there are only two: (1) foundationalist theories[2] and (2) coherence theories.

Foundationalist Theories

Foundationalist theories of knowledge get their name from the structure they attribute to our body of knowledge. According to the foundationalist, our knowledge can be seen as something of a pyramid. At the base we have various foundational beliefs, and it is from these foundational beliefs that we *reason* our way to our other beliefs. In this way the foundational beliefs serve to support all our other beliefs. In other words, epistemic justification flows upward from these foundational beliefs to the rest of our beliefs.

Of all the theories of knowledge, foundationalism seems to best accord with our common sense view of how we attain knowledge. First it recognizes that most of our knowledge of the world comes to us empirically through our senses. Our senses are what provide us with our foundational beliefs. Foundationalism also recognizes that we can and do give reasons for holding particular beliefs about the world, but that eventually these reasons come to an end; we can go no further. Thus foundationalism is not threatened with any kind of infinite regress of epistemic justification, because we eventually end up at a foundational belief which admits of no further, noncircular justification. This too seems to accord with common sense. When pushed to justify some belief we hold about the world, reasons eventually fail us (or we end up repeating reasons we have already adumbrated). Generally, these final reasons that we are pushed to seem to enjoy some special epistemic status; they do not stand in need of justification. The foundationalist refers to these beliefs as *basic beliefs* and accords them a privileged, self-justifying, epistemic status (e.g., self-evident, certain, indubitable, incorrigible). They serve as the *foundation* for all our other knowledge, and all our other knowledge can be somehow derived from these basic beliefs.

The central tenets of foundationalism are thus twofold. (1) There are some empirical beliefs, *basic beliefs*, which do not stand in need of epistemic justification. They do not depend on any other beliefs but are in some way self-justifying. (2) All our other empirical knowledge is ultimately justified by these basic beliefs. Through some chain of reasoning we can derive all of our empirical knowledge from these basic beliefs. These two tenets, in turn, translate into two tasks which any foundationalist theory must attend to. Corresponding to (1), the foundationalist must identify and account for her basic beliefs. What are they and how is it that they are self-justifying? Corresponding to (2), the foundationalist needs to address the problem of epistemic ascent. She must explain how these basic beliefs serve as the ultimate source of epistemic justification for all our other beliefs. How is it that we reason from the basic beliefs to the nonbasic beliefs?

While both issues are critical to the success of any foundationalist theory, how do they relate to my skeptical concerns? The first issue, the identity and nature of basic beliefs, relates most closely to the skeptical argument I identified in chapter 3. If there are such things as empirical, self-justifying, basic beliefs, their existence would cast doubt on the skeptic's assertion (premise 1 of the skeptical argument) that the experiences of a person have true perceptual beliefs could be the same as the person having false perceptual beliefs. If the fact that a belief is self-justifying (a basic belief) or justified by a chain of reasoning from basic belief is a mark that the belief is true (i.e., these characteristics of beliefs are truth-conducive), then having these characteristics would be a way of distinguishing true perceptual beliefs from false. In this way the first premise of the skeptical argument is shown to be false. Of course for this antiskeptical move to work, we need to know more about basic beliefs and how they are self-justifying. We need to know what constitutes a basic belief (i.e., how we are to identify them), and how it is that basic beliefs are truth-conducive. This second question constitutes the requirement for metajustification demanded by the skeptic.

What then are the candidates for the foundationalist's basic beliefs? They generally are perceptual beliefs, but not what we might ordinarily think of as perceptual beliefs. For example, the belief that there is a red book before me will not count as a basic belief. It does not enjoy the kind of privileged epistemic status that a basic belief ought to have. For example, I could be mistaken about the color of the book or mistaken that it is a book at all (it might be a clever drawing of a book). However, what I cannot be mistaken about, according to the foundationalist, are my sensory experiences, the way things appear to me. Even if I am dreaming, I still will know how it is things appear to me. It is these "appearing to" beliefs, then, that generally constitute the foundationalist's basic beliefs. They are beliefs about which I cannot be mistaken and from which all my other beliefs about the external world are justified.[3]

Despite its initial plausibility, foundation theories have been criticized from a number of different perspectives. I will look at but a few of these objections with the aim of showing how they lead to what I consider the main skeptical objection to foundationalism. I begin with Pollock's main argument against foundationalism. He starts by offering the following argument:

(1) We rarely have beliefs about how things "appear to" us.
(2) Only such beliefs are plausible candidates as basic beliefs (especially given the dream hypothesis). Therefore,
(3) Perceptual knowledge is not based on basic beliefs and hence foundationalism is false.[4]

Although Pollock's argument is apparently valid, his premises rest on a confusion. While it may be true that we rarely entertain beliefs about how things appear to us, it is not because of some genetic intellectual shortcoming on our part. It is merely a matter of practical, cognitive expediency. We move so quickly from how things appear to us to our beliefs about the external world that we generally do not entertain "appearing to" beliefs. Only when circumstances dictate, e.g., when we have reason to doubt certain of our beliefs about the external world, do we make the distinction between how things appear to us and how they really are.

When we are doing theory of knowledge in philosophy, we *are* in circumstances which dictate entertaining beliefs about how things appear to us, and we are all able to entertain those kinds of "appearing to" beliefs. The skeptic gives us reason to doubt our knowledge of the external world, and one route for denying the skeptic's claim is by appeal to how things appear to us. So while it may be the case that we do not often entertain "appearing to" beliefs when formulating our everyday, run-of-the-mill beliefs, we can and may entertain such beliefs when we are interested in justifying those everyday beliefs. How one arrives at a belief and how that belief is justified are two distinct issues. Pollock attacks foundationalism on the basis that it does not accord with our understanding of how our beliefs arise. But the foundationalist is interested in how our beliefs are justified regardless of their genesis. Within this context an appeal to "appearing to" beliefs as basic beliefs surely is legitimate. Only if Pollock could show that we are unable to entertain such basic beliefs would his argument be successful.

He does attempt to make such an argument, but I believe it too fails. While Pollock admits that we can direct our attention inward so as to become aware of our having sensory experiences, he maintains that this is different from having beliefs about those experiences. By his account we rarely or never even entertain such beliefs about the content of our sensory experiences. Though we can become aware of having a sensory experience, we never or rarely have an idea of the "very complicated abstract pattern that constitutes that sensory experience." As an example he cites the "discovery made fairly early by every landscape painter is that snow looks blue (particularly the shadows). Most people think snow looks white to them, but they are wrong."[5]

But what exactly does this show and how does it save Pollock's argument? Before the landscape painter makes his discovery he will wrongly describe his sensory experience when he looks at snow as "white." Based on that wrong description he will hold the false belief that his sensory experience appears white to him. Later, by painting a number of snowscapes, he will make the discovery that he has misdescribed his sensory experience, and that when he believed he was sensing white he was actually sensing blue. If he had no beliefs about his sensory experience when perceiving snow, how could he have made the discovery that his sensory experience was really blue and not white? We may make a mistake and misdescribe our sensory experience, but in the final analysis we really do know our own sensory experience (or how else could we discover the mistake).

Even Pollock admits that we can go beyond mere awareness of our sensory experience to awareness of the "complicated pattern that constitutes that sensory experience," and hence a belief about that pattern.

With considerable training one can become aware of some of these patterns. Acquiring such awareness is an important part of becoming a painter, but it is a difficult process.[6]

As long as such awareness, even though difficult, is at least possible, the foundationalist's appeal to "appearing to" beliefs as basic beliefs seems legitimate. The most Pollock has demonstrated is that the epistemic justification of beliefs for the foundationalist is a difficult process that requires considerable training and sensory awareness. He has not demonstrated that "appearing to" beliefs do not exist, as he must if his argument against foundationalism is to succeed. However, Pollock's argument does begin to open the door to another, and I believe more serious, objection to foundation theories. This objection concerns the alleged truth-conduciveness of basic beliefs and what I have thus far characterized as misdescribing our sensory experience. However, I will approach this objection from a slightly different angle by examining the antifoundationalist arguments of Laurence BonJour.

In *The Structure of Empirical Knowledge*, Laurence BonJour offers the following argument against foundation theories. He is concerned with establishing the truth-conduciveness of the foundationalist's standard of epistemic justification, i.e., the metajustification for foundationalism. According to BonJour, any argument for the basicness of a given type of belief will likely be of this form:

(1) Belief *B* (the alleged basic belief) has characteristic *c* (where *c* is the characteristic that marks off a belief as properly basic).
(2) Beliefs with *c* are highly likely to be true. Therefore,
(3) *B* is highly likely to be true (i.e., *B* is a basic belief).[7]

However, claims BonJour, premise 1 must be an empirical premise as *B* is, by hypothesis, an empirical belief. But then *B* is not properly basic as it depends on one empirical belief for its justification. The foundationalist has violated his own definition of a basic belief. The beliefs that *B* has *c* and that beliefs with *c* are highly likely to be true are epistemically prior to the basic belief *B*. This argument seems to be saying that a belief is basic only if it is not basic. Therefore, BonJour concludes, there can be no basic empirical beliefs, and hence, foundation theories are false.

What is important to note here is that BonJour attacks foundationalism at the level of metajustification. The argument he finds fault with is essentially a metajustificatory argument. It is an argument designed to demonstrate that a certain type of belief (one with characteristic *c*) is in fact true or highly likely to be true, i.e., it is a basic belief. Such a metajustificatory argument is necessary, according to BonJour, because it is not enough to identify what beliefs are properly basic, but the foundationalist must also demonstrate that basic beliefs are highly likely to be true. He looks at the foundationalist's standard for epistemic justification (appeal to basic beliefs) and critically assesses how one might demonstrate that this standard leads to true beliefs. He argues that we may know *a priori* that beliefs with a certain characteristic *c* are likely to be true, but the foundationalist still must demonstrate that her basic beliefs do in fact possess characteristic *c*—and this is necessarily an empirical matter. Otherwise she cannot get to the conclusion, demanded by the requirement for metajustification, that the alleged basic belief is highly likely to be true. But if the foundationalist must appeal to some empirical justification to demonstrate that a basic belief is true, then by definition of what it means to be a basic belief, the belief in question cannot be basic.

But there is a sense in which such a requirement seems unfair. If *B* is properly basic, then its very nature is such that it needs no further justification, and that includes any metajustification. The very nature of a basic belief obviates the requirement for metajustification. When confronted with a properly basic belief we cannot help but realize that it is basic and therefore true. Further empirical justification of the sort imagined by BonJour is simply unnecessary.

This rejoinder to BonJour's argument relies on what he calls the "doctrine of the empirically given." The strategy here is to argue that certain beliefs, namely, properly basic beliefs, are "empirically given" to us and do not stand in need of further justification. The goal of such a doctrine is to separate out—in the case of basic beliefs—the need for justification from the ability to confer justification. What the foundationalist is first striving to identify is a special set of beliefs for which the demand for further epistemic justification is illegitimate. Secondly, these very same beliefs must be such that they can be legitimately used as a source of epistemic justification for all our other empirical beliefs. Such a separation, however, does not seem possible.

As BonJour correctly points out, the problem for this doctrine of the given is twofold. In order for the "given" basic belief to possess the ability to confer justification it must be a cognitive state of some sort (an intuition, an apprehension, an immediate experience). No matter how primitive, if it is a cognitive state, it will have some representational content—even if the nature of that cognitive state can hardly be expressed in language (e.g., a dark form has entered my visual field, my skin is being lightly touched). To use the language of John Locke, this belief/cognitive state will involve both sensation and reflection, however brief and transitory, on the sensation.[8] And that reflection will involve a judgment concerning what the sensation might represent. Yet, if the belief in question does have some representational content, the question of whether that representation is correct or *true* can still legitimately arise. The requirement for further justification is not averted.

However (and now we are moving to the second problem for defenders of the doctrine of the given) if we pare away what is "given" to the point where it needs no further justification, the ability to confer justification is seriously compromised. If the given belief has no representational content, if it is merely some sort of raw sense data, in what sense is it a belief at all? Such a "belief" would appear to have no real content such that it could serve as the grounds for justifying other empirical beliefs. If the concept of the "given" is understood in this way, it becomes a concept that is just too slim to confer justification. Thus, the foundationalist is faced with a dilemma. That characteristic which accords to the "given" its ability to confer justification (representational content) is the same characteristic which raises the question of further justification. The two cannot be separated from each other. What we discover in the end is that the doctrine of the given does not avert the need for metajustification. The hope that it can is, in BonJour's words, "indeed a myth."[9]

However, if "givenness" does not solve the foundationalist's problem with metajustification, there is yet another route she may fruitfully pursue. It may be the case that basic beliefs are known to us *a priori*. As such, a properly basic belief will need no further justification because of its *a priori* nature. This is the strategy Chisholm seems to adopt in discussing what he calls the "directly evident."[10] If basic beliefs are directly evident to us *a priori*, the requirement for further justification for them seems strange at best. When I claim that "this appears white to me," what more can I offer in the way of justification for that claim than that "I believe that this appears white to me." To question this latter claim seems absurd as I have *a priori* knowledge of my own beliefs. Beyond this point the demand for metajustification is unneeded; it can serve no purpose.

BonJour explains the foundationalist's appeal to the *a priori* as follows.[11] As you will recall, the problem with the metajustificatory argument attributed to the foundationalist concerned the first premise: (1) belief *B* (the alleged basic belief) has characteristic *c* (where *c* is the characteristic that marks off a belief as properly basic). This premise can be supported by the following two propositions:

(a) *B* has as its subject matter a purported description of my present experience. (*B* has *c*.)

(b) *B* is accepted by me now. (I believe *B*.)[12] The parenthetical notes are mine.

The claim is that both premises are known *a priori* so that even though the foundationalist's original metajustificatory argument depended on an empirical premise (premise 1 above), this premise is in turn supported by *a priori* reasoning which does not need any further justification. The regress of justification ends and foundationalism is vindicated.

Unfortunately, the problem of metajustification is not so neatly solved. What is at question here is premise b: I believe *B*. But surely this is an odd question. I know by experiencing *B* that I accept *B*. What could be more certain than this? However, as BonJour points out, there is a distinction to be made between experiencing B and believing oneself to be experiencing B.[13] The foundationalist who appeals to the *a priori* is presupposing that the two are the same when they are not. The content of the first state (experiencing B) is simply B, while the content of the latter belief is more complex and involves a belief about that experience. A belief about an experience, unlike a mere experience, involves some sort of description of the experience (at least to oneself), and it clearly seems possible that we might misdescribe our experience.

The earlier example from Pollock involving landscape painters and blue snow is one such example. Another illustration of this kind of misdescription comes from an experience of one of my friends. While on a trip with his sister he observed a hallway in the hotel they were staying at and came to the belief, based on his sensory experience, that the wall in the hallway was gray. When his sister and several bystanders pointed out to him that it was really blue, he realized his error and changed his belief appropriately. Assuming, as he claims, that my friend is not color blind and that his observation of the wall was under ideal conditions, his experience did not change as he went from believing the wall was gray to believing it was blue. His belief, though, clearly did change, in much the same way that the landscape painter's belief changed from the belief snow is white to the belief snow is blue. Furthermore, the error involved in this misdescription of experience is not merely a verbal or linguistic error. In both cases, the painter's and my friend's, there is no confusion concerning the meaning of the words being used to describe the color of the snow or the wall.

Now what does all this talk of belief versus experience portend for the foundationalist's claim that basic beliefs are known *a priori*? From the examples above it is clear that the purported basic belief in question (B is accepted by me or I believe B) cannot be known *a priori*. To begin with, necessity is a mark of the *a priori*. As my examples make clear, the beliefs in question are not necessary but contingent. On the other hand, I will concede that, unlike our beliefs concerning our experiences, there is no possibility of error concerning our experiences themselves. But from this we cannot presuppose that there is anything in the external world that corresponds to this experience. In going from experience to belief about that experience, there is no guarantee that the belief will be true. As with the doctrine of the given, mere states of experience are too slim a concept to provide justification for our other empirical beliefs. It is not that experience is empty of content, it is just that raw experience, uninterpreted and unanalyzed, is not rich enough to confer epistemic justification on our beliefs. Furthermore, such an appeal to this kind of experience in no way addresses the dream hypothesis postulated by the skeptic's argument. If, as the skeptic's examples are meant to show, it is logically possible that the experiences of a person having a true perceptual belief and the experiences of a person having a false perceptual belief are indistinguishable, then using unanalyzed, uninterpreted experience as the foundation for all of our empirical knowledge simply begs the skeptical question.

In the end, despite its initial plausibility, the theory of foundationalism fails to address the skeptic's theoretical concerns. I have examined foundationalism first, however, because I feel it comes the closest to adequately answering the skeptic. The other theories I will look at largely developed out of the failure of foundationalism to succeed as an adequate theory of knowledge. In my opinion, however, these theories face even greater difficulties, and in the end I will have reason to return to foundationalism. But first let us examine the other doxastic theory: coherence theory.

Coherence Theories

Coherence theories, like foundationalism, accept the *doxastic assumption* that the only thing that can serve as epistemic justification for our beliefs is other beliefs. Where the two theories differ is in the epistemic status they assign to beliefs. While the foundationalist believes that a certain subset of our beliefs (i.e., basic beliefs) enjoys a privileged epistemic status, the coherence theorist attributes the same epistemic status to them all. There are no foundationalist beliefs upon which the rest of our knowledge is built. Instead, in the words of Otto Neurath, "we are like sailors who must rebuild their ship upon the open sea."[14] We start with a certain set of beliefs, and then we add to and delete from this set based on some epistemic standard which is itself a part of our overall doxastic state. We don't have the luxury of starting from scratch, laying a firm foundation, and then building up our edifice of knowledge. For if we begin, in the manner of Descartes, by setting aside all our putative knowledge, we will not be able to get started again. It is this idea, nicely captured in Neurath's metaphor, that is central to all coherence theories.

If there are no epistemically privileged beliefs from which we can infer all of our other beliefs, how is it that beliefs are justified in coherence theory? For the coherence theorist, justification is the result of a certain kind of relationship holding between the belief or beliefs in question and all our other beliefs. A belief is epistemically justified if it *coheres* with our other beliefs. This relationship of coherence takes many different forms, but generally a belief *coheres* with our overall body of beliefs (our *doxastic state*) if accepting the belief in question does not lead to a contradiction in our overall *doxastic state* or the belief can be inferred from our other beliefs.

Coherence theories are generally classified into two main types: linear or nonlinear. A linear theory sees epistemic justification as a series of inferences. Belief that P is justified by the belief Q, which in turn is justified by the belief R, and so on. Eventually, if this regress of justification is not to continue infinitely, the coherence theorist argues that the sequence of justification circles back on itself. However, if the circle of justification is wide enough, goes the argument, this circularity is not vicious. Clearly, however, this argument seems suspect, for no matter how wide the circle of justification, our justification for the belief that P is seen to depend, eventually, on P itself. For this reason, among others, most coherence theories adopt a nonlinear view of justification.

According to this nonlinear or *holistic* view of justification, a belief is justified not by appeal to a sequential series of beliefs but by appeal to one's entire doxastic state. In other words, the coherence relationship is viewed from within the context of all of one's beliefs. On such a holistic view of justification, we are more concerned with systematic coherence among all of our beliefs rather than coherence among particular beliefs in that system (although, of course, the former will entail the latter). A succinct way of expressing this difference is that in a holistic theory we will most naturally speak of "having reason" for holding a belief, whereas in a linear theory we will speak of "having *a* reason."[15]

The type of coherence theories I will be concerned with here are the holistic coherence theories. My reasons for this are twofold. First, with respect to the skeptical argument, linear theories seem by far the weaker of the two general types. No matter how large the circle of justification is construed to be, linear coherence theories are ultimately circular. Such circular reasoning will clearly not satisfy the skeptic. Second, these two concepts of justification, linear and holistic, correspond to two different issues raised by the skeptic. The first issue involves the justification of a single or small number of empirical beliefs within the framework of an already accepted and apparently justified system of beliefs. At this "local" level of justification, our justificatory argument will appear largely linear in nature. However, a further question may yet be raised concerning the justification of the entire system of beliefs, that body of beliefs upon which justification at the local level ultimately depends. In raising this issue we are now concerned with a more "global" level of justification. At this level, any successful justificatory argument offered by a coherence theorist can no longer be linear in nature. Such a linear justification depends upon the presumption that there already is a justified system of beliefs in place. But in raising the global issue of epistemic justification, it is this very presumption that is being questioned. Therefore, whatever justificatory argument the coherence theorist might offer, it will be holistic in nature relying, as it must, upon a system of mutual and interdependent support that exists among all the beliefs in one's belief system, rather than some epistemically privileged foundational belief.[16]

It is this second, global issue of justification, necessarily holistic in nature for any coherence theory, which is my primary concern. Of the two questions, local and global, it is the most fundamental. Any coherence theory of knowledge must address this global issue if it is to be successful. Failure to do so merely begs the question raised by the skeptic. For these reasons I will largely limit my discussion of coherence theories to holistic coherence theories.

Holistic coherence theories themselves can be further classified into two different categories: negative and positive. Negative coherence theories begin with the *presumption* that all our beliefs are epistemically justified. From this presumption, our justificatory arguments function in a negative manner. Rather than providing the epistemic standards which ought to apply in acquiring new beliefs, the epistemic standards provided by negative coherence theories tell us when we are justified in *rejecting* a belief. The presumption at work here is that all beliefs are epistemically innocent until proven guilty.

Once again, however, it is this very presumption that the skeptic is challenging. Moreover, the skeptic has provided reason to believe that our beliefs (in this case our beliefs about the external world) are in fact suspect. They all may be the product of our dreams and have no connection with the real world. To answer the skeptic's indictment of our beliefs by merely denying his conclusion, which is essentially what the negative coherence theory does, is once more a form of question begging. Such a move simply does not prove persuasive.

Positive coherence theories, on the other hand, do not rely on the epistemic presumption of innocent until proven guilty. Instead they require a justificatory argument in support of each and every one of our beliefs. The standards of justification they provide are meant to function as normative standards for belief *acquisition* and not merely belief rejection. In this regard, positive, holistic coherence theories, like foundationalism, seem to properly recognize the force of the skeptic's argument. However, they too run into problems in dealing with the requirement for metajustification.

In general, the standard objection to any coherence theory of knowledge revolves around how one's system of beliefs hooks up to the truth. One can come up with any number of coherent belief systems, but there is no guarantee that this system of beliefs will be true. How is it that coherence as an epistemic standard leads one to true beliefs about the external world? A common way to answer this question is by appeal to perception. Perception is the conduit by which input from the external world is brought into a person's system of beliefs. How perception is to serve this purpose often involves a long and complex series of arguments, but the point is, it is this input which connects our system of beliefs with the external world. However, even if we allow perception into our picture of how beliefs about the external world are justified, significant skeptical problems involving the requirement for metajustification remain.

To better understand these problems it seems useful to go back to an earlier argument offered against foundationalism and the possibility that there were such things as properly basic beliefs. This argument, taken from BonJour, asserted that any argument for the basicness of a given type of belief would be of this form:

(1) Belief B (the alleged basic belief) has characteristic c (where c is the characteristic that marks off a belief as properly basic).

(2) Beliefs with c are highly likely to be true. Therefore,

(3) B is highly likely to be true.

Now if we understand B to represent any empirical belief and c to represent the epistemic standard of coherence, i.e., belief B coheres with one's total system of beliefs and perceptual inputs, the above argument becomes a metajustificatory argument for coherence theories in general. However, for such an argument to work premises 1 and 2 must themselves be justified. But how is the coherence theorist able to justify these premises? Presumably this will happen by an appeal to c or she will violate and raise doubts concerning her own epistemic standard of coherence. Having c is not enough though. In the case of premises 1 and 2 we must also be justified in believing: (1*) they have characteristic c, and (2*) by having c they are highly likely to be true. But then we must justify 1* and 2*. You can see the regress that results. Substitute any characteristic for c that you like and the problem faced by any metajustificatory argument of this type becomes clear.

What this points out is something I noted in the last chapter. Any argument for metajustification must necessarily be *a priori*. If premises 1 and 2 stand in need of further justification, an infinite regress seems to be the result. Now premise 2 may be *a priori*, but premise 1 seems clearly to be a contingent, empirical belief. But in order to avoid an infinite regress, premise 1 must not stand in need of further justification. However, it is not open to the coherence theorist to argue that premise 1 does not stand in need of further justification. Doing so would accord premise 1 a privileged epistemic status, something which contradicts coherence theory. To avoid the regress is to return to a foundations type theory. But, as we have seen in the preceding section, foundationalism also fails the requirement for metajustification. The only beliefs that may plausibly serve as basic beliefs are too slim to confer justification on the rest of our beliefs. In eliminating the need for further epistemic justification of a belief, we are left with a concept that is not rich enough to do the work of epistemic justification.

Perhaps the problem lies in the *doxastic assumption* with which I began this chapter. Both foundation theories and coherence theories subscribe to the assumption that epistemic justification for everything we know about the world depends *entirely* upon what beliefs we hold—our *doxastic state*. It may be the case that if we jettison this assumption, the skeptic's argument may yet be defeated. Is it possible that something other than one's beliefs can serve as epistemic justification? I turn to that possibility in the next chapter.

Notes

1. John Pollock, *Contemporary Theories of Knowledge* (Totowa, N.J.: Rowman & Littlefield, 1986), 19–25.
2. Foundationalist theories need not be doxastic; however, most traditional foundationalist theories, which are the ones I intend to examine here, are doxastic.
3. See Roderick Chisholm, *Perceiving* (Ithaca, N.Y.: Cornell University Press, 1957), for more on "appearing to" beliefs as basic beliefs.
4. Pollock, *Contemporary Theories of Knowledge*, 61–64.
5. Pollock, *Contemporary Theories of Knowledge*, 63.

6. Ibid.

7. Laurence BonJour, *The Structure of Empirical Knowledge* (Cambridge: Harvard University Press, 1985), 31–33.

8. John Locke, *An Essay Concerning Human Understanding*, ed. Alexander C. Fraser (New York: Dover, 1959), book II, chapter 1, sections 3–4.

9. BonJour, *The Structure of Empirical Knowledge*, 79. For more on BonJour's argument against the doctrine of the given see chapter 4, especially sections 4.2–4.4.

10. See Roderick Chisholm, *Theory of Knowledge* (2nd ed. [Englewood Cliffs, N.J.: Prentice-Hall, 1977]), especially chapter 3. Not all "directly evident" beliefs are known *a priori* by us according to Chisholm. Appearance beliefs, which he labels the "first truths *a posteriori*," require experience to arise in the first place, but once our experiences give rise to these appearance beliefs, no further appeal to experience is needed to justify them. They are justifiable *a priori*.

11. BonJour, *The Structure of Empirical Knowledge*, 82.

12. Ibid.

13. BonJour, *The Structure of Empirical Knowledge*, 27 and 83.

14. Quoted in Pollock, *Contemporary Theories of Knowledge*, 67.

15. Pollock, *Contemporary Theories of Knowledge*, 73.

16. See BonJour, *The Structure of Empirical Knowledge*, 90–93, for more on this local/global distinction.

Chapter Five

Nondoxastic Theories of Knowledge

The apparent problems inherent in doxastic theories of knowledge have motivated some to propose theories which deny the doxastic assumption. As will be recalled, the doxastic assumption asserts that epistemic justification for everything one knows about the world depends *entirely* upon what beliefs one holds—the subject's doxastic state. One's beliefs, and only one's beliefs, play a role in epistemic justification. Nondoxastic theories reject this assumption. For these theories, epistemic justification is a function of more than just the beliefs of the putative knower. Exactly what additional factors they allow into the process of epistemic justification permit nondoxastic theories to be further classified into two main types: externalist theories and internalist theories.

Internalist theories claim that epistemic justification is a function of one's internal states. Since beliefs are internal states, all doxastic theories are necessarily internalist theories. However, there are other internal states, e.g., intuitions, mental images, uninterpreted perceptual states or memory states, that may not have the status of a belief. A belief is generally conceived as the holding of a proposition to be true. As such, a belief is an internal state which has a fairly rich content. But there are other internal states which may not be so rich in content as a belief. Theories which allow these more primitive states to play a role in epistemic justification remain internalist theories, but they are nondoxastic. I will address this type of internalist, nondoxastic theory later in this chapter, but right now I want to focus on externalist, nondoxastic theories.

Externalist Nondoxastic Theories

Externalist theories are motivated by the following *aporia:*[1]

(1) Epistemic justification is a function of the putative knowers beliefs/internal states.

(2) A putative knower's internal states do not provide sufficient justification for knowledge of the external world.

(3) We have knowledge of the external world.

The only way out of an *aporia* such as this is to reject one of the three claims. Rejecting 3 while accepting 1 and 2 leads to skepticism. Rejecting 2 while accepting 1 and 3 is the internalist position. However, based on the previous chapter we have reason to reject 1. If beliefs are the only internal states that can play a role in epistemic justification, then the arguments in chapter 4 seem to indicate that, contrary to 3, we can have no knowledge of the external world. If we are to accept 3, we are forced to reject 1 and embrace 2. This is the strategy adopted by the externalist. The externalist's claim is that internal states do not provide sufficient justification for knowledge of the external world, yet we do possess such knowledge. Therefore it must be something external to the putative knower which justifies our knowledge of the external world.

The externalist claim, in very simplified form, seems to be something like the following. The externalist recognizes the need for justification if one is to regard a belief as knowledge. However, the justification need not be something the putative knower is aware of. This seems, at first examination, to be a very strange claim at best. I can know something even though I cannot, and may never be able to, give the reasons which justify my claim to knowledge. Now it may be that the externalist means to reject the whole traditional conception of epistemic justification and knowledge (perhaps even rationality),[2] but assuming that is not the case, what does an externalist theory look like? I will briefly look at two recent externalist theories with the aim of affording them some plausibility before I press my arguments against them.

Robert Nozick offers the following analysis of knowledge.

S knows *p* if and only if:

(1) *p* is true,

(2) *S* believes that p,

(3) If *p* weren't true then *S* would not believe that *p*, and

(4) If *p* were true then *S* would believe that *p*.[3]

Nozick calls this theory the tracking theory of knowledge, and his third and fourth criteria constitute what he calls the tracking conditions. As he describes the theory,

[t]o know is to have a belief that tracks the truth. Knowledge is a particular way of being connected with the world, having a specific real factual connection to the world: tracking it.[4]

However, the fact that a belief tracks the truth is not something that the subject need be cognizant of. This tracking relationship is something external to the subject, yet it is essential in justifying the subject's knowledge of *p*.

Now if this tracking solution were correct, it would clearly block the skeptic's dream argument. To see this Nozick applies his theory to the question: how do we know that the skeptic's conditions, e.g., the dream hypothesis, do not obtain.

S knows that the skeptic's conditions (*Sk*) do not hold if and only if:

(1) *Sk* doesn't hold,
(2) *S* believes *Sk* doesn't hold,
(3) If *Sk* were to hold, *S* *wouldn't* believe *Sk* doesn't hold, and
(4) If *Sk* were not to hold, *S* would believe it does not.[5]

Of course, the skeptic attacks 3 by constructing examples such that if *Sk* were to hold, *S* *would* believe *Sk* doesn't hold. But if Nozick can show that such examples do not threaten the truth of 3, he will have won the day. He does this by denying the *closure principle*.

The *closure principle* is the claim that if you know *p*, and you know *p* entails *q*, then you know *q*. The skeptic uses the *closure principle* to make the following argument:

Assume:
(A) *S* knows *p* [where *p* represents some knowledge claim].
(B) *S* knows (*p* entails not-*Sk*) [from A and our definition of knowledge].
(C) *S* knows not-*Sk* [from A and B and closure principle]. But,
(D) Not-(*S* knows not-*Sk*) [by hypothesis]. Therefore,
(E) Not-(*S* knows *p*) [from B and D].

Nozick's rejoinder to this argument adopts the strategy of denying the *closure principle*. According to him one can know *p*, know if *p* then *q*, and *not* know *q*. Applied to the skeptical argument, one can know *p*, know if *p* then the skeptic's conditions do not obtain, and *not* know that the skeptic's conditions do not obtain. When it comes to knowledge claims the *closure principle* assumes that our beliefs will remain the same when not-*p* is true and when the skeptic's conditions obtain. But this assumption is simply false, and the tracking conditions of Nozick's theory demonstrate this. If the skeptic's conditions really did obtain, then none of us, including the skeptic, would know that the skeptic's conditions obtain. This is why so many skeptical philosophers (here Nozick cites Hume as an example) are unable to maintain their skeptical beliefs all the time.[6]

Before looking at arguments against Nozick's version of externalism, I would like to outline another externalist theory, the *reliabilist* theory of Alvin Goldman. As I believe both theories suffer from many of the same shortcomings, it seems wise to get each of them out in the open before attempting any skeptical refutation.

Goldman's theory is comprehensively presented in his book *Epistemology and Cognition*.[7] The general idea behind the theory is that a belief is justified if and only if it is formed by a reliable process. For Goldman this process is based on a series of rules, such that his theory could be labelled *rule reliabilism*.[8] There is a three-tiered structure to his reliabilism, the first tier being what he calls the *Framework Principle*. According to this principle, a justified belief is any one permitted by a right system of justificational rules or *J-rules*. Of course this Framework Principle is neutral as to what constitutes a right system of rules. We must move to the next two tiers for more specifics.

What makes a J-rule system right is if it results in a high truth ratio. And how do we know which rules ought to be permitted into our J-rule system? The answer, according to Goldman, lies in the cognitive sciences, the third tier of his theory. Logic alone cannot give these rules to us, so we must turn to cognitive science for the answer. This is what he calls his connection thesis, the idea that the specifics of a right J-rule system must be given to us by cognitive science. Once cognitive science discovers these right J-rules, we will understand how our knowledge is possible, namely, it is the result of these right rules/processes (rules which result in a high ratio of true beliefs) licensing our beliefs. But once again, since Goldman's is an externalist theory, the putative knower may not be aware that his beliefs are being formed by the right (or wrong) system of J-rules. Only we, as outsiders looking on, can make that determination.

Now there is a sense in which these two externalist theories have answered the skeptic. They do tell us *how* the knowledge we seem to possess is possible. If a belief tracks the truth or is formed by a right system of J-rules, it is a case of knowledge. But does this knowledge help the putative knower determine whether he himself possesses knowledge? Can the account of knowledge given by the externalist be used by each of us to determine the epistemic warrant of our *own* beliefs? If the externalist's criteria are beyond the knower's ken, the answer seems to be no.

However, I'm not so sure any externalist theory is aimed at providing an account of knowledge that is normative in nature, i.e., gives individual knowers criteria they can apply to justify their *own* beliefs. Both Nozick and Goldman are fairly explicit on this point. Nozick begins his book by making a distinction between philosophical argumentation, which is coercive in nature, and explanation, which is noncoercive. He characterizes the former as the "foreign relations" department of one's belief system, that part of our belief system which we use to convince others to accept certain beliefs. Explanation is aimed at solving domestic type problems, e.g., how is my knowledge possible. It is the "internal affairs bureau" of one's belief system. As such, explanation may often involve hypotheses which are unknown to the subject himself. A theory of knowledge, insofar as it involves explanation about how knowledge is possible, can make use of externalist criteria of which the individual subject of knowledge may be unaware.[9]

Goldman develops a similar line of thought. For him, "justificational rules are understood as tools of theoretical appraisal, not as regulative principles."[10] Therefore, the internalist requirement that epistemic justification be something the subject is able to appeal to and is aware of, is not a necessary component for a theory of knowledge. Again this seems to license externalist criteria of epistemic justification. It also contrasts with Pollock's view in which epistemic standards of justification must be reason-guiding with the goal of attaining true belief. Externalist standards of justification, in that they are not available to the knower, except retrospectively, cannot be reason-guiding, and for this reason they are rejected by Pollock.[11] But if the externalist does not see it as part of his goal to provide first-person belief justification, how can we criticize the theory on its failure to accomplish this goal?

There are at least two criticisms that I believe soundly refute any externalist theory. The first centers on two questions posed by Ernest Sosa:

(Q1) How is it possible for me to know that *h*?
(Q2) Given that I do know that *h*, *how* do I know such a thing?[12]

We want to know not only how knowledge is *possible*, but what knowledge is *actual* for *me*. Externalist theories, in that they fail to answer the question of actual knowledge (Q2), are unsatisfactory. While this criticism may sound a bit like Pollock's complaint against externalist theories, there is a difference. Making use of Nozick's distinction between argumentation and explanation, the externalist has more explaining to do. First-person belief justification is important to us (or we wouldn't feel the force of Descartes' dream argument), and any theory of knowledge which ignores the question of first-person belief justification is incomplete.

The externalist might attenuate this criticism in the following manner. Externalist theories do answer the question of first-person belief justification, but in an indirect manner. By observing and researching how people come to acquire beliefs, we can then inductively infer which processes for belief formation are the most reliable/truth-conducive. However, the only way we will discover these right processes is from a third-person perspective. The first-person perspective is simply too narrow to judge the reliability of a belief-forming process. But once we have discovered these processes, we can use them ourselves for the formation of our own beliefs with a high assurance that they will lead to true beliefs.

Such a response merely pushes the question of first-person belief justification one level higher. How do I know I am using reliable/truth-conducive processes when I look at other's belief forming processes from my third-person perspective? How will Goldman's cognitive scientist know when he has discovered the *right* J-rule system? As Stroud points out, the externalist is making the following type of claim:

> I don't know if I understand human knowledge or not. If what I believe about it is true and my beliefs are produced in what my theory says is the right way, I do know how human knowledge comes to be, so in that sense I understand. But if my beliefs are not true, or not arrived at in that way, I do not. I wonder which it is. I wonder whether I understand human knowledge or not.[13]

Surely this is not a satisfactory account of knowledge!

Contrary to Goldman's view above, I think the best that can be said for externalism is that it may have some practical, regulative merit, but as a theory it seems utterly bankrupt. When it comes to epistemic justification, it does seem true that we are often reduced to using externalist-type criteria, standards of common sense which rely on factors beyond the subject's perspective. This may turn out to be the best we can do, but a theory of knowledge, if it is to defeat skepticism, cannot leave it at that.[14]

The problem, once again, is one of metajustification. The externalist comes up with standard of epistemic justification which he claims to be truth-conducive. However, it is truth-conducive only if the process he uses to come up with this standard is truth-conducive. But the truth-conduciveness of his process is the very thing in question. To answer this question on the basis of the very process in question, is simply so much question-begging. It would be very much like asserting, if I know I'm not dreaming then I know I'm not dreaming *and* I know I'm not dreaming. Therefore, I know I'm not dreaming. In the end, externalist theories of knowledge prove to be no real threat to the skeptic's argument.

Another Variety of Externalism

However, before moving on to consider internalist nondoxastic theories, I would like to examine one more variety of externalism that recently has been proposed by Alvin Plantinga.[15] Plantinga's externalist theory rests on a distinction he draws between *warrant* and *justification*. Warrant, as he defines this concept, is that which, along with truth, is sufficient for knowledge. Warrant is concerned with the evidence for a belief and is essentially an objective (i.e., nonsubjective) concept. Justification, at least as that concept has been traditionally understood, has something to do with our epistemic duty. Believing something without the appropriate epistemic justification constitutes a failure to fulfill one's intellectual duty. Justification on this view must be a subjective concept (which is to say, something internal to the knowing subject) in that it is concerned with what grounds or evidence the individual knower has available to him or her, and thus can be held culpably responsible for.

In order to better understand this distinction between warrant and "deontological" justification (Plantinga adds the deontological modifier to stress the intellectual duty component of justification) Plantinga draws an analogy with moral duty. Here the distinction is between a person's subjective moral duty as opposed to their objective moral duty. Objective moral duty is a person's, all-things-considered moral obligation. However, failure to accomplish one's objective moral duty does not necessarily subject one to moral censure or blame. Circumstances do not always permit one to consider all things in deciding what moral duty demands. Sometimes people are ignorant of important facts bearing on their moral decision making. For reasons such as these, persons normally are considered morally blameworthy only if they *knowingly* fail to do their moral duty. That is to say, appropriate moral blame only attaches to violations of subjective moral duty.

However, as Plantinga points out, for a very large class of cases, subjective moral duty and objective moral duty coincide. In many, many cases ignorance is no excuse for failing to accomplish one's objective moral duty. While the person failing to do what objective moral duty demands may claim that he did not know his actions were wrong or that he was in some sense unable to do any better, we often do not accept such explanations. You should have known better; you should have tried harder. This is often our response to these kinds of situations because we believe that subjective and objective moral duty, more often than not, are identical.

Returning now to epistemic matters, Plantinga wonders if there is not an analogous relationship between warrant and justification. Is it the case that justification, the fulfilling of our epistemic/intellectual duty, is both a necessary and sufficient criterion for warrant?[16] Certainly that has been the traditional view in epistemology (going back to at least Descartes and Locke, as Plantinga convincingly argues). But is it the correct view? Plantinga thinks not.

The problem is, according to Plantinga (and as the skeptic's arguments make clear), justification can fall woefully short of providing warrant for some (perhaps many or all—depending on your degree of skepticism) of our beliefs. Furthermore, the insufficiency of justification for warrant seems independent of the knower's epistemic scrupulousness in forming beliefs. No matter how careful someone may be in examining and reflecting on their beliefs, if they are subject to something like Descartes' dream hypothesis, their beliefs have no warrant. And yet, if they have done all they *could* do in the fulfillment of their epistemic duty, in what sense do they merit censure—in what sense are they deontologically unjustified? Perhaps the concept of justification needs to be divorced from deontology? Perhaps the traditional linking of justification with epistemic/ intellectual duty is simply wrong? At least this is what Plantinga claims.[17]

But then, if we divorce justification from intellectual duty, what motivation is there for retaining an internalist conception of justification? For that matter, perhaps the whole concept of epistemic justification should be overthrown? If the question of epistemic justification fails to establish that the subject has fulfilled his or her epistemic duty and, in addition, is not sufficient for warrant, the whole issue of warrant and justification requires an overhaul. Plantinga proposes that warrant no longer be understood in terms deontological justification, i.e., in terms of doing one's epistemic duty or of absolving one of blame for one's beliefs. Instead, warrant should be a matter of "proper functioning" by the subject. As he puts it, a belief has warrant for me only if, among other things,

> it has been produced in me by cognitive faculties that are working properly (functioning as they ought to, subject to no cognitive dysfunction) in a cognitive environment that is appropriate for my kinds of cognitive faculties.[18]

However, what warrant is *not* is some sort of internally verifiable cognitive state of the subject. In this respect Plantinga's theory is an externalist theory, and it seems to me, still does not answer the skeptic's charges. What counts as a properly functioning cognitive faculty? Who makes this determination if it is not the knowing subject? How does this outside party know that *her* cognitive faculties are functioning properly when making the determination that the knowing subject's faculties are functioning properly? The problem here is very much like the problem I have already addressed in discussing Goldman's system of J-rules. There the question was how will Goldman's cognitive scientist know when he has discovered the right J-rule system. Now the question is how does the external observer in Plantinga's theory know when she has discovered what constitutes the proper functioning of our cognitive faculties.

Plantinga does have an answer of sorts—he appeals to the notion of design. One's cognitive faculties are functioning properly when they are functioning *as designed*. The notion of design, of course, assumes a designer, and this designer (the theistic God) is the external observer for Plantinga. Nonetheless, this appeal to theism leaves unanswered the core of the skeptic's question: *how* do *I* know anything? It is that first-person question concerning knowledge—*how* do *I* know?—that is at issue here. It may well turn out, as Plantinga has argued (and as my investigation has thus far shown), that justification will not be sufficient for warrant. But if that is the case, why not embrace skepticism rather than discard the traditional, and highly intuitive, concept of *internal*, epistemic justification. The turn to an externalist theory of knowledge seems to only make sense if we see the alternative of skepticism as some kind of nonsense. But I have yet to see a convincing argument, from Plantinga or anyone else, that the skeptical alternative is nonsense.

Now, I will have reason to revisit this issue and Plantinga's variety of externalism when I discuss the issue of *naturalized epistemology* in chapter 7. For the present, however, I would like to turn to an examination of another type of nondoxastic theory.

Internalist Nondoxastic Theories

Internalist nondoxastic theories represent the other category of theories which deny the doxastic assumption. Pollock's theory of *direct realism* is an example of such a theory (and is the only one I am aware of). Pollock arrives at this theory through a process of elimination. If neither externalist theories nor doxastic theories can defeat skepticism, the only option Pollock sees available is an internalist theory which does not depend entirely on the putative knowers beliefs to serve the function of justification. What he formulates is a theory which allows one to make direct inferences from perceptual states to physical-object beliefs. Accordingly, his claim is that in formulating rules of epistemic justification, we "must be able to appeal directly to our being in perceptual states and need not appeal to our having beliefs to that effect."[19]

To this end, Pollock formulates two kinds of epistemic connections. On the one hand we can have fully doxastic connections between beliefs while at the same time allowing half-doxastic epistemic connections between beliefs and nondoxastic states. For example, the fact that I am in the perceptual state of being appeared to redly and roundly can give me epistemic justification for believing there is a tomato before me. There is no need for the mediating belief that *I am being appeared to redly and roundly*. We rarely entertain such beliefs and they generally serve no important function. What this gives us is a kind of foundationalist theory with basic mental states at the foundation rather than basic beliefs.

However, this sounds too much like the foundationalist's appeal to the *a priori* which I discussed in chapter 4. I will concede that, unlike our beliefs concerning our mental states, there is no possibility of error concerning these states themselves. The fact that I am in a certain perceptual state is just that, a fact. No error is possible, so there is a sense in which the mental state itself does not stand in need of further justification. But from this we cannot presuppose there is anything in the external, physical-object world that corresponds to this perceptual state. As with the doctrine of the given (also discussed in chapter 4), there is just not enough content to a mental state to provide the kind of justification we need to get from that mental state to a belief about the external world. Raw experience or perception, uninterpreted and unanalyzed, is simply not rich enough to confer epistemic justification on our beliefs. Epistemic justification requires some judgment as a justifying premise, and judgment requires analysis of the raw data of experience. Furthermore, if raw experience is to be the foundation upon which the edifice of knowledge is built, it is the truth-conduciveness of that very foundation which the skeptic's argument is meant to undermine. His examples are designed to show that we have no way of distinguishing true perceptual beliefs from false perceptual beliefs on the basis of experience or mental states alone. Against this argument, Pollock's *direct realism* seems powerless.

At this point one might be compelled to wonder how any of these nondoxastic theories came to be proposed in the first place. They seem either entirely implausible or hopelessly question-begging. The answer lies in an assumption made at the beginning of Pollock's book—the skeptic cannot be right. He sees the skeptic's argument as a reductio ad absurdum and the problem for epistemology is to demonstrate how the skeptic's reasoning has gone wrong. The question is not *do we know anything* but rather *given that we do know things*, how is that knowledge possible. This is very much like the approach adopted by G. E. Moore in many of his papers and lectures. By examining his arguments, and how they succeed and fail, I think we will come to a better appreciation of skepticism. The skeptic's argument is not meant to be taken as a reductio ad absurdum. To do so is not only mistaken but represents a degree of intellectual negligence as well.

Notes

1. An *aporia* (Greek for "puzzle") is a set of propositions that are individually plausible but collectively lead to inconsistency. I got the idea of using aporetic sets from Nicholas Rescher, "Aporetic Method in Philosophy" in *Review of Metaphysics* 41 (December 1987): 282–97.

2. Laurence BonJour briefly discusses this possibility in *The Structure of Empirical Knowledge* (Cambridge: Harvard University Press, 1985.), 35 and 56.

3. Robert Nozick, *Philosophical Explanations* (Cambridge: Harvard University Press, 1981), 172–78.

4. Nozick, *Philosophical Explanations*, 178.

5. Nozick, *Philosophical Explanations*, 200–4.

6. Nozick, *Philosophical Explanations*, 204–10, for greater detail on Nozick's argument.

7. Other sources on Alvin Goldman's theory of reliabilism include "Strong and Weak Justification" in *Philosophical Perspectives*, vol. 2, edited by James Tomberlin (Atascadero, Calif.: Ridgeview Publishing Co., 1988) and "Precis and Update on *Epistemology and Cognition*" in *Knowledge and Skepticism*, ed. Marjorie Clay and Keith Lehrer (Boulder, Colo.: Westview Press, 1989). I draw on all three sources in outlining Goldman's views.

8. This is a label Ernest Sosa attaches to Goldman's theory. See Sosa's "Beyond Skepticism to the Best of our Knowledge" in *Mind* 97 (April 1988): 164.

9. Nozick, *Philosophical Explanations*, Introduction.

10. Goldman, "Precis and Update," 70–71.

11. John Pollock, *Contemporary Theories of Knowledge* (Totowa, N.J.: Rowman & Littlefield, 1986), 133–38.

12. Sosa, "Beyond Skepticism," 156.

13. Barry Stroud, "Understanding Human Knowledge in General," in *Knowledge and Skepticism*, ed. Marjorie Clay and Keith Lehrer (Boulder, Colo.: Westview Press, 1989), 47.

14. BonJour makes a similar point in *The Structure of Empirical Knowledge*, 52.

15. See Alvin Plantinga's two recent books, *Warrant: The Current Debate* (New

York: Oxford University Press, 1993) and *Warrant and Proper Function* (New York: Oxford University Press, 1993), for a more detailed explanation of his theory. The first book focuses on why the traditional concept of epistemic justification needs revision; the second focuses on his own theory of proper function.

16. Plantinga argues that justification is neither necessary nor sufficient for warrant. In my remarks I will address only the *insufficiency* of justification for warrant.

17. In support of this claim, Plantinga cites William Alston as someone who is especially clear on the need to reform the traditional understanding of justification. See in particular, Alston's "Concepts of Epistemic Justification" (*The Monist* 68 [January 1985]: 57–89) and "An Externalist's Internalism" (*Synthese* 74 [March 1988]: 264–83).

18. Plantinga, *Warrant and Proper Function*, 46.

19. Pollock, *Contemporary Theories of Knowledge*, 173. For more on Pollock's theory of direct realism see his *Knowledge and Justification* (Princeton: Princeton University Press, 1974).

Chapter Six

Moore's Argument from Common Sense

In examining Moore's arguments concerning our knowledge of the external world, I intend to focus mainly on those arguments expressed in two of his papers—"A Defense of Common Sense" and "Proof of an External World."[1] These two papers seem to most clearly illustrate his position against skepticism. I want to look at Moore's arguments because I think they most clearly exhibit one of the major flaws in many of the arguments marshalled against skepticism. If we understand the skeptic's stance vis-à-vis Moore's argument, and why the skeptic finds his argument unconvincing, we will come a long ways toward understanding the nature of the skeptical viewpoint.

Moore's argument, in both papers, begins in essentially the same way. He starts by giving the reader examples of what he himself knows, examples he believes his readers will also know or think they know. According to Moore, these "truisms" are things he knows with certainty. Some examples that he gives us include, "There exists at present a living human body, which is *my* body . . . born at a certain time in the past, and has existed continuously ever since."[2] He then goes on to assert that he knows, with certainty, that most other human beings know these same things about themselves. In "Proof of an External World" he starts with a similar claim. First he gestures with his right hand and then with his left and argues from the alleged truism, "Here is one hand and . . . here is another."[3] From these premises, examples of things he knows with certainty, he goes on to prove the existence of external things. For if we *know* that there exists two hands or *know* there exists a living human body, it seems clear that we *know* there exists an external world—a conclusion which seems incompatible with the skeptical position. However, there seems to be something a little peculiar about the examples Moore uses. For the argument to work he has to use examples that appear above question. They have to be examples his audience or readers will accept as certain knowledge. There can be no possibility of doubt when considering these propositions. But on what basis are these alleged truisms beyond doubt? Furthermore, if they are beyond doubt, if the very possibility of doubt is denied, doesn't this beg the question against the skeptic? And if they are question begging examples, in what way are they philosophically interesting?

Yet, if Moore were to use examples about which there might be some doubt (e.g., Newburgh, New York, is situated on the west bank of the Hudson River, General George Custer is buried in the West Point Cemetery, the Sears Tower in Chicago is the tallest building in the world), the examples no longer do the work they were intended to do. His examples are the premises for his conclusion that he *knows* there exists an external world. His proof would not be a good one unless, as he points out,

> the premiss which I adduced was something which I *knew* to be the case, and not merely something which I believed but which was by no means certain, or something which, though in fact true, I did not know to be so. . . .[4]

Not only must Moore know these premises to be true, but if the proof is to be at all convincing, most of his audience must know these premises to be true as well. And Moore thinks this is the case with the examples he has chosen. That is why he has chosen them, and that is why he accords them the status of "truisms."

Moore's truisms do, in fact, seem to enjoy some special status. They are contingent truths, but they appear to exhibit an unusual kind of certainty. For one thing, they are entailed by related pairs of apparently contradictory propositions. For example, the proposition, *I am six feet tall,* and its negation, *I am not six feet tall,* each seem to entail Moore's truism, "*there exists at present a living human body, which is my body.*" Likewise, the proposition, *I am wearing a glove on my left hand,* and its negation, *I am not wearing a glove on my left hand,* each seem to entail the proposition, *I have a left hand.* When seen in this light, Moore's examples give the impression they are necessary truths, but this cannot be correct. The existence of my living body or the fact that I have a hand is surely a contingent matter.

There are, however, other problems with these kinds of proofs for Moore's truisms. First, and most obvious, the premises (the related pairs of contradictory propositions) seem to presuppose the truth of the conclusions. In fact, it is only if there is such a presupposition that the entailment from these premises to his truisms holds. This leads directly to the second problem. The pairs of propositions which entail Moore's truisms are not really contradictories but rather contraries.

If they were true contradictories we would be able to derive Moore's truism from a constructive dilemma proof. However, from the disjunctive proposition, *I am wearing a glove on my left hand, or I am not wearing a glove on my left hand,* one may *not* necessarily conclude that *I have a left hand.* Rather, it may be the case that *I have no left hand* (I may have been born without a one or lost it in an accident). The point here is that while both of the disjuncts above cannot be true, they both could be false. In such a case (where both of the contrary propositions are false) the constructive dilemma proof of Moore's truism is unsound. Similar reasoning can be applied to Moore's other truisms. But third, and most importantly, these proofs are not Moore's own. In fact, as he makes clear, he is offering no proof for any of his truisms. In responding to those who might object to his argument because he has not proven the truth of the premises (i.e., he has not proven that "here is one hand and here is another"), Moore comments:

> I can know things, which I cannot prove; and among things which I certainly did know, even if (as I think) I could not prove them, were the premisses of my two proofs. I should say, therefore, that those, if any, who are dissatisfied with these proofs merely on the ground that I did not know their premisses [because he cannot prove their truth], have no good reason for their dissatisfaction.[5]

For Moore, the truth of these premises—his truisms—stands above proof.

The question can still be asked, however, what makes our knowledge of these propositions so secure? And if it is so secure, what does the skeptic find wanting in Moore's proof? There seems to be one main idea (or a number of closely related ideas) at work in these proofs, an idea which I believe demonstrates the unsatisfactoriness of Moore's response to the skeptical question. To begin with, he is approaching the whole issue from a different perspective than the skeptic. His argument, like Pollock's, is a kind of reductio ad absurdum. If the skeptic's analysis of knowledge (*how* we know certain things) conjoined with rational argumentation entails the conclusion that we have no certain knowledge of the external world, such a conclusion is absurd. The problem is not that we have no knowledge of the external world; our common sense tells us we do. The problem is we have no good analysis of *how* such knowledge is possible.

> And this is a matter as to which I think I differ from many philosophers. . . . Many, . . . while holding that there is no doubt as to their *analysis*, seem to have doubted whether any such propositions are *true*. I, on the other hand, while holding that there is no doubt whatever that many such propositions are wholly true, hold also that no philosopher, hitherto, has succeeded in suggesting an analysis of them, as regards certain important points, which comes anywhere near to being certain.[6]

And because this analysis is missing, the skeptic still has cause to doubt. Moore presumes we have certain knowledge of his truisms, but can offer no analysis of the meaning of the propositions which express his truisms, e.g., *here is a hand*. Yet, if we understand these truisms as making some sort of knowledge claim, the skeptic's demand for some analysis of their meaning does not seem unreasonable. And part of that analysis must include, if it is to answer the skeptical challenge, an answer to the question, *how do you know here is a hand*. Without such an analysis, the skeptic's doubts seem only half-answered at best.

Stroud, in his discussion of this issue, seems to view it in a similar sort of way. Moore's reaction to skepticism is what Stroud calls an "internal" reaction. It is internal because "it is a response 'within' one's current body of knowledge."[7] The question of whether I know a certain thing is merely a question of whether or not it is part of my current body of knowledge or can somehow be coherently included in my current body of knowledge. The skeptic, on the other hand, views the problem of knowledge from an "external" perspective according to Stroud. From this perspective:

> I am to focus on my relation to the whole body of beliefs which I take to be knowledge of the external world and ask, from "outside" it, as it were, not simply whether it is true but whether and *how* any of the things I admittedly do believe are things that I know or can have reason to believe (my emphasis).[8]

Because of this difference of perspective—internal versus external—Moore never really connects up and addresses the skeptical argument. For this reason the skeptic is left unsatisfied—and rightly so.

Moore as much as admits his refusal to even acknowledge the skeptical claim that we have no knowledge of the external world. According to him the skeptic is looking for a proof of something that Moore sees no need for.

> How am I to prove now that "Here's one hand, and here's another?" I do not believe I can do it. In order to do it I should need to prove for one thing, as Descartes pointed out, that I am not now dreaming. But how can I prove that I am not? I have, no doubt, conclusive reasons for asserting that I am not now dreaming; I have conclusive evidence that I am awake; but that is a very different thing from being able to prove it.[9]

It seems to me that the best way to understand Moore's refusal on this point is as a conflict or paradox involving rational, abstract reasoning on the one hand and common sense on the other hand. Moore sides with common sense; the skeptic sides with abstract reasoning.

Common sense tells us that Moore's truisms are examples of certain knowledge. They have no need of proof. We can deny their truth only in the abstract. However, rational argument at the abstract level leads us to deny the truth of these common sense propositions. We seem left on the horns of a dilemma, a dilemma which Hume acknowledged some 200 years earlier. As Hume puts it:

The chief objection against all *abstract* reasonings is derived from the ideas of space and time; ideas, which, in common life and to a careless view, are very clear and intelligible, but when they pass through the scrutiny of the profound sciences (and they are the chief object of these sciences) afford principles, which seem full of absurdity and contradiction. . . . But what renders the matter more extraordinary, is, that these seemingly absurd opinions are supported by a chain of reasoning, the clearest and most natural.[10]

In wrestling with this dilemma, Hume offers us a solution of sorts. The skeptic must remain in his "proper sphere" when displaying his "*philosophical objections.*" To venture outside of this sphere and expose his principles to the light of common life is to cause these skeptical principles to "vanish like smoke, and leave the most determined sceptic in the same condition as other mortals."[11]

So for Hume, abstract reasoning and its skeptical concerns occupy one realm of inquiry while the common sense concerns of everyday life occupy a different realm of inquiry. Now while Hume has more to say on this topic, and how these two realms might interact, I will postpone discussion of that until a future chapter. At present there are only two main points I wish to take away from this discussion of Moore's "proofs." First, Moore, as I hope I have adequately shown, does not really address the skeptical question I am concerned with in any kind of forthright manner. Instead, he leaves us with a paradox in which abstract, rational argumentation contradicts our common sense. He accepts the common sense view as correct, but gives us little in the way of argumentation for that view. Furthermore, he doesn't tell us what is wrong with our abstract reasoning concerning the nature of knowledge. *How* is it that our common sense knowledge is possible? Second, our examination of Moore's argument has brought out the two-sided nature of the issue. Depending on one's perspective—internal and abstract or external and commonsensical—the skeptic's doubts will seem more or less relevant. How we should view these different perspectives and how they impact on one another will be the subject of much of the rest of this work.

Overview

We are now at the point where we can begin to examine some of the more radical solutions to skepticism. However, before beginning our exploration of these solutions, it seems helpful to briefly go over how we got here. Doing so will serve two purposes. First, it will be a useful summary and will hopefully tie some things together. Second, and more importantly, the solutions offered by post-analytic philosophy really only make sense against the backdrop of failure provided by the more traditional theories of epistemology. If we are to give post-analytic solutions a charitable hearing, we must keep in mind the context in which they have developed.

Underlying all the theories of knowledge I have so far examined, is an attempt to answer one of two closely related questions. On the one hand we want to discover the extent of our knowledge—what do I know? In addition, we want to know *how* it is that we know what we know—what are the criteria for knowledge?[12] The questions are interrelated in that if we can answer either one we should be able to answer the other. This then gives us two approaches for dealing with the philosophical problem of knowledge. If we can determine what it is we know, we can then use that knowledge to figure out how it is we know these things. Conversely, if we can determine how we come to certify certain beliefs as knowledge, we can use the standards or criteria we come up with to figure out the extent of our knowledge.

Moore begins by answering the first question—what do we know. According to him we know many things: there is an external world, there exists a living body which is my body, here is a hand, etc. Then, given that we know these many things, the work of epistemology is to figure out how it is that we know them, i.e., come up with the criteria for this knowledge. Philosophers who believe, like Moore, that the best approach in epistemology involves answering the first question (what do I know?) and then working out the answer to the second (how do I know?) are what Chisholm calls "particularists." Philosophers who work in the opposite direction—discover the criteria of knowledge and then figure out the extent of our knowledge—he calls "methodists."[13]

Most of the theories I have examined are best characterized as particularist theories. The foundationalist, the coherentist,[14] the internalist, and the externalist all begin with the belief that they have the answer to the first question (and their answer would undoubtedly be very similar to Moore's). That is why they see the skeptic's argument as a reductio ad absurdum and reason as follows. "I know a great many things, e.g., *p*, *q*, and *r*. If I know *p* and *q* and *r*, then clearly the skeptic's argument has gone wrong. If his argument has gone wrong, then the only task remaining is to show how his argument has gone wrong. I can only do that by using what I do know to figure out the correct criteria for knowledge."

But it is at just this point that the skeptic makes his reply. In the tradition of Hume and Descartes, the skeptic is a methodist: "Give me your criteria of knowledge, how it is that we know things, before you tell me what you know." He attempts to force the antiskeptic back to the methodist question with his demand for metajustification. "If these are your criteria for knowledge, show me how your criteria are truth-conducive" And it is just at this point, as we have seen, that the antiskeptic fails. Virtually any metajustificatory argument that she can come up with does not withstand the scrutiny of the skeptic. The foundationalist's basic beliefs are either not properly basic, or they are too slim to confer justification. Much the same sort of arguments can be brought to bear against other internalist theories. What is internal to the knower is either not rich enough to confer epistemic justification on our other beliefs or stands in need of further justification itself. Externalist theories beg the metajustificatory argument even more blatantly. If what is internal to the subject cannot confer epistemic justification, claims the externalist, then let us leave the limited perspective of the subject and adopt an external, third-person perspective. Now while this third-person perspective, especially if we assume some sort of God's-eye point of view, is almost certain to guarantee the truth-conduciveness of our criteria for knowledge, it does so at a steep price: first-person epistemic justification. And as I hope I have adequately shown in the previous chapters, it is the first-person perspective which is crucial to the problem of knowledge.

Because of these problems at the level of epistemic metajustification, most theories resist the skeptic's conclusions by avoiding these issues altogether and adhering to the particularist's strategy. To do otherwise and adopt the methodist's strategy seems to doom the antiskeptic from the beginning. In a sense Kant, with his Copernican revolution, was one of the first to recognize the necessity of adopting the particularist stance. If I understand his project correctly, the "scandal to philosophy" which so troubled him was not that no proof for the existence of the external world had yet been given, but that anyone should see the need for such a proof.

Kant's aim was to reject the presumption upon which the skeptic's arguments are based, namely, the appearance-reality distinction. It is this distinction that leads one to doubt our knowledge of the external world. If human knowledge is at all possible, claims Kant, then we must have direct, noninferential access to the external world. The objects of the external world must be somehow "in us." This is what Kant's thesis of transcendental idealism seems to be all about. As he puts it:

> In order to arrive at the reality of outer objects I have just as little need to resort to inference as I have in regard to the reality of the objects of my inner sense, that is, in regard to the reality of my thoughts. For in both cases alike the objects are nothing but representations, the immediate perception (consciousness) of which is at the same time a sufficient proof of their reality.[15]

Clearly then, in Kant's view, we know many things about the external world. The problem is explaining how such knowledge is possible, and the only way it is possible is if transcendental idealism is true. Note, however, that Kant, like Moore, begins with the presumption that we do have knowledge, *direct knowledge*, of the external world.

> The transcendental idealist is, therefore, an empirical realist, and allows to matter, as appearance, a reality which does not permit of being inferred.[16]

But, by presuming such direct access to reality, Kant, again like Moore, seems to begin by presuming the very knowledge that the skeptic gives us cause to doubt.

And now we are face to face with the skeptical dilemma. If we adopt the particularist strategy in doing epistemology, we end up assuming the very thing the skeptic gives us cause to doubt, i.e., knowledge of the external world. If we adopt the methodist strategy in doing epistemology, we are in a position where the truth-conduciveness of our method can never be fully settled, and the skeptic appears to win the day. It is within the context of this unhappy dilemma that post-analytic solutions to skepticism make their appearance. Their solution involves nothing less (and nothing more as will be seen) than a refusal to entertain the skeptical problem altogether.

Notes

1. Both these papers are found in George E. Moore's *Philosophical Papers* (New York: Humanities Press Inc., 1959), 32–59 and 127–50, respectively.

2. Moore, *Philosophical Papers*, 33.

3. Moore, *Philosophical Papers*, 146.

4. Ibid.

5. Moore, *Philosophical Papers*, 150.

6. Moore, *Philosophical Papers*, 53.

7. Barry Stroud, *The Significance of Philosophical Scepticism* (New York: Clarendon Press, 1984), 117.

8. Stroud, *The Significance of Philosophical Scepticism*, 118.

9. Moore, *Philosophical Papers*, 149.

10. David Hume, *An Enquiry Concerning Human Understanding*, ed. Eric Steinberg (Indianapolis: Hackett Publishing Co., 1977), 107–8.

11. Hume, *An Enquiry Concerning Human Understanding*, 109–10.

12. These two questions, and the problems they pose for epistemology, are the subject of Roderick Chisholm's "The Problem of the Criterion" in *The Foundations of Knowledge* (Minneapolis: University of Minnesota Press, 1982), 61–75.

13. Chisholm, "The Problem of the Criterion," 66.

14. Coherentist theories may be seen as methodist theories as well. They begin with a method for warranting knowledge claims, viz., coherence, and then go on to determine exactly what they know using coherence as their warrant. I actually believe the process of developing a coherence theory generally takes a particularist approach (I know all these things, now what marks them off as cases of knowledge?—they cohere). In either case, the coherentist must still answer the question of metajustification as I point out below.

15. Immanuel Kant, *Critique of Pure Reason*, trans. Norman K. Smith (New York: St. Martin's Press, 1965), A371.

16. Kant, *Critique of Pure Reason*, A371.

Chapter Seven

Post-Analytic Solutions to Skepticism

The post-analytic solution to skepticism is a fairly recent and novel approach in epistemology. While post-analytic philosophers would no doubt object to my labeling their position as a "solution" to skepticism, their views do render moot the skeptic's arguments. However, the specifics of their position are somewhat difficult to grasp without understanding what they are reacting to and against. In order to understand these specifics, I believe we must begin with the arguments of Kant.

The Kantian Roots of Post-Analytic Philosophy

In many ways, the move to post-analytical kinds of solutions in the realm of epistemology can be seen as a reaction to Kant's argument in the *Critique of Pure Reason*. As I noted in the previous chapter, his position involved a rejection of the appearance-reality distinction, but this rejection can be seen to come at the price of reality. Although somewhat simplistic, Kant sums up his entire argument in the *Critique of Pure Reason* in two paragraphs in his *Prolegomena to Any Future Metaphysics*.

> Since the oldest days of philosophy, inquirers into pure reason have conceived, besides the things of the sense, or appearances (*phenomena*), which make up the sensible world, certain being of the understanding (*noumena*), which should constitute an intelligible world. And as appearance and illusion were by those

men identified (a thing which we may well excuse in an undeveloped epoch), actuality was only conceded to the beings of the understanding.

And we indeed, rightly considering objects of sense as mere appearances, confess thereby that they are based upon a thing in itself, though we know not this thing as it is in itself but only know its appearances, namely, the way in which our senses are affected by this unknown something. The understanding, therefore, by assuming appearances, grant the existence of things in themselves also; and to this extent we may say that the representation of such things as are the basis for appearances, consequently of mere beings of the understanding, is not only admissible but unavoidable.[1]

What Kant is proposing here is a kind of revolution in thinking analogous to the revolution Copernicus incited when he placed the sun at the center of the universe rather than the earth. Instead of asking how our knowledge corresponds with the real world (i.e., how what appears to us matches reality) Kant proposes that we begin with the supposition that the objects of the real world *must* conform to our knowledge. Although I am not nearly as eloquent as Kant, I would summarize his argument as follows:

(1) Our inquiries into reason lead us to view the world as constituted of *phenomena* (appearances, the sensible world) and *noumena* (actuality, the thing in itself, the intelligible world).

(2) It is a mistake to identify the *noumenal* world with the *phenomenal* world and grant actuality to the *noumenal* world alone, because all our knowledge comes from appearances (the *phenomena*).

(3) The basis or ground of appearance is the *noumenal* world.

(4) Of this *noumenal* world, the things in themselves, we can have no knowledge.

(5) Nonetheless it is unavoidable for us, as thinking beings, to grant existence to the *noumenal* world and think about it as the basis of appearance.

Now while Kant does not outright reject the *noumenal* world (what I have been calling the external world), his thesis of transcendental idealism clearly favors the world of appearance. This emphasis on appearance (in fact neo-Kantians generally begin by rejecting the *noumenal* world) naturally leads to a new emphasis on the subject's perspective and how that perspective contributes to what is real. Truth as correspondence to the external, *noumenal* world begins to look like a mistaken concept, and the whole project of philosophy is set on a new course. The tensions upon which the skeptic bases all of his arguments—appearance/reality, internal/external, subjective/objective, value/fact—are seen as pointless. Reality or truth as an external, objective fact gives way to internal, subjective appearance and judgments of value.

But I am getting ahead of myself here. Besides Kant, there are a number of other philosophers that contributed to the rise of post-analytic philosophy. While I do not mean to offer anything close to a complete history, by understanding some of the strands of thought that feed into the post-analytical, hermeneutical view of epistemology, we should be able to make better sense of the position they advocate. Also, as this is not a history, I will be somewhat brief and only offer my own summaries and interpretations of many important philosophical positions. Since they are only summaries, they are no doubt incomplete on many points and may not represent the final view of any of these philosophers. What seems important, however, are the ideas themselves (even if they are incomplete and arguably inaccurately attributed) and how they gave momentum to the post-analytic movement in philosophy.

Wittgenstein and Quine

I begin with Wittgenstein and the impact of his philosophy on our view of language. Linguistic philosophers began with the idea that a careful study of language could resolve many of the problems facing philosophy. From such a study we will come to see that these problems rest largely on the imperfections of our language. Therefore, philosophy's task is to come up with an ideal language which will help us see these problems as they really are, i.e., as resting on some sort of linguistic confusion. In the realm of epistemology, the ideal language will demonstrate to us how knowledge of the external world is possible by showing us how our language hooks onto that world.

In his earlier philosophy, the *Tractatus Logico Philosophicus*, Wittgenstein attempts to accomplish just such a task with his "picture theory" of knowledge. The idea behind the picture theory is that language depicts the logical structure of facts in the world and the *Tractatus* represents Wittgenstein's attempt to establish what the logical form of that language must be in order to accomplish this depiction. On his view, words have meaning in that they name something; primitive names refer to primitive objects. These names, when arranged in a sentence, paint a picture of things in the world. This is how language hooks onto the world: through the *naming* relationship. This is a kind of correspondence theory of meaning which dovetails nicely with a correspondence theory of truth.

However, in the *Philosophical Investigations* Wittgenstein comes to realize that language is much more complicated than he originally had thought. The theory of language which he developed in the *Tractatus* was only one of a multitude of ways a language could be understood. He compares language to a game and concludes that the naming game is only one of the many language games that might be constructed. Meaning and understanding in a language are more than merely a matter of naming.

> For a *large* class of cases—though not for all—in which we employ the word
> "meaning," it can be defined thus: the meaning of a word is its use in the
> language.[2]

Wittgenstein's new view of language, in which the meaning of words depends on their use, calls into question the whole enterprise of the *Tractatus*. Linguistic philosophy can no longer be seen as a quest for an ideal language for new language games can be added indefinitely. As Wittgenstein puts it "it is clear that every sentence in our language 'is in order as it is.' That is to say, we are not *striving after* an ideal, as if our ordinary vague sentences had not yet got a quite unexceptional sense, and a perfect language awaited construction by us."[3] The idea of a correct form, logic, or meaning is itself no longer meaningful. There is no all-encompassing criteria of understanding to which we can appeal; there is no one correct way in which language hooks onto the world.

Moreover, even if we were able to construct an ideal language, it may not be of any practical use according to Wittgenstein.

> The more narrowly we examine actual language, the sharper becomes the
> conflict between it and our requirement [the requirement of the ideal
> language]. . . . The conflict becomes intolerable; the requirement is now in
> danger of becoming empty.—We have got onto slippery ground where there is
> no friction and so in a certain sense the conditions are ideal, but also, just
> because of that, we are unable to walk. We want to walk: so we need *friction*.
> Back to the rough ground![4]

If meaning in a language is tied to the "rough ground" of use and there are indefinitely many uses for a language (some of which are incompatible), the key question for Wittgenstein becomes how is it possible that we are able to communicate with each other. What is it that provides the necessary determinacy in a language to enable communication? For Wittgenstein, one of the key concepts that make up a language game and provides the necessary determinacy for language is agreement between persons in a society. Agreement consists of certain common and shared practices within a community of people. For without such agreement, language itself would be impossible. This agreement is not so much agreement of opinions as it is agreement in a certain "form of life." "It is what people *say* that is true and false; and they agree in the *language* they use. That is not agreement in opinions but form of life."[5] It is not explained by the fact that all members of a given community grasp some sort of objective truth about the world they find themselves in. Rather it is merely an agreement about the rules and objectives of a particular language game (rules and objectives that may change over time or as the community changes).[6]

From Wittgenstein's *Investigations* there seem to be two conclusions one might draw concerning how language hooks onto the world: (1) language hooks onto the world in indefinitely many ways and there is no *single* correct way, or

(2) language does not hook onto the world at all, language is all merely a matter of convention. If we accept (1) as the correct conclusion, and I believe this is the correct conclusion, Wittgenstein's *Investigations* is largely seen as an attack on philosophy of language. His assertion seems to be that a close study of language, the search for an ideal language, will not give us the kind of foundational knowledge of the external world that we are searching for. Language is not suited to such a task as it is not based on such a foundations view of knowledge. Rather language rests principally on agreement as to "forms of life," where form of life manifests itself in use, action, and behavior. The "therapy" that philosophy is meant to provide us comes from the realization that "linguistic philosophy" cannot, in the end, resolve the questions of epistemology and metaphysics for us. Only when we grasp this lesson will our "bewitchment" with language end.[7]

Accepting (2) as the correct conclusion to be drawn from Wittgenstein, we come to a very different kind of view. Rather than seeing the *Investigations* as an attack on philosophy of language, we can interpret it as a refutation of sorts of skepticism. The refutation takes this general form. Language does not hook onto the external world, i.e., the truth of a language claim is not determined by how that claim represents things as they are in the objective world. The only thing that language does hook onto and what gives language any determinacy is agreement as to "form of life," i.e., one's form of life and how language conforms to that form of life is what makes a language claim true or false. Whatever truth there may be in our language claims is truth within the framework of some form of life, and not a kind of objective truth that lies outside of this community framework. Therefore, the kind of truth the skeptic seeks, objective truth about the external world, is in some sense meaningless, and hence the skeptic does not present us with a real problem.

On this interpretation, Wittgenstein's attack on philosophy of language has been turned into an attack on the nature of truth, which is largely what the post-analytic move in philosophy is all about. The skeptic's arguments become implausible if we give up the traditional goal of philosophy as a rational endeavor aimed at discovering the truth. With no objective truth to discover, what can the skeptic's point possibly be?

Quine makes a related point concerning language and use in his essay "Ontological Relativity."[8] With Wittgenstein, he agrees that our use of language depends on rules, but it also depends on the nature of things in the world. But what counts as the nature of things is not independent. Our *judgments* about what there is in the world and their nature are always embedded in some theory. We can never completely detach ourselves from some theory in making our judgments. There is no objective, value-free perspective available to us. What we take to make up our world depends on what theory we bring to our inquiries, and this choice of theory, in turn, reflects some sort of value judgment on our part.[9]

If Quine is correct, and I think he largely is on this point, then it seems that knowledge of the world as an objective, value-free entity (Kant's *noumenal world*) is forever beyond our reach. And if this is the case, one could (mistakenly I believe) draw the further conclusion that epistemology's goal of discovering the *objectively true* nature of the world is misguided.

In each of these interpretations of Wittgenstein's and Quine's arguments (or by my view, a degree of misinterpretation of their arguments), the skeptic is being attacked on the ground that there is something wrong or misguided in his conception of truth. But the arguments of Wittgenstein and Quine were not the only ones that seemed to favor a reinterpretation of the truth and its relation to the goals of philosophy. Other arguments also seem to point us in a similar direction.

Putnam on the Value-Fact Dichotomy

One of the distinctions that the skeptic trades heavily on is the value-fact dichotomy. The skeptic's argument only makes sense against the backdrop of an objective, mind-independent, external world. Without such a world to discover, the world of objects and facts, skepticism loses its bite. But then the question arises: Is there such a world, an objective, mind-independent, external world, or is it merely a concept constructed from our imagination? Putnam argues that the existence of such a world, what he calls the thesis of metaphysical realism, is highly problematic. As appealing and plausible as metaphysical realism may seem, there is no escaping, even in our imagination, the realm of values. In developing our theories of knowledge, theories that claim to demonstrate how it is we know the facts of the external world, of necessity we make judgments of value. The value-fact dichotomy (championed by Moore and his naturalistic fallacy) simply does not hold up to close scrutiny. It is an imagined dichotomy.[10]

Putnam's thesis is that "every fact is value loaded and every one of our values loads some fact."[11] One cannot choose a conceptual scheme or a theory of knowledge which straightforwardly copies the facts. Any choice of conceptual scheme presupposes values of a certain sort.[12] Especially relevant to epistemology is a theory of truth. But even our theory of truth presupposes a theory of rationality which presupposes our theory of good. And, of course, a theory of good depends upon value judgments concerning human nature, society, and the nature of the universe. As our values change our world view, so too does our theory of good change, which in turn can affect our theories of rationality and truth. As a result of these considerations Putnam concludes that "there is no such thing as a foundation" in philosophy; there is no Method of philosophy.[13]

Such a conclusion might seem to support a radical sort of relativism, or even skepticism. Putnam thinks not. However, the most we can hope for is "to produce a more rational *conception* of rationality . . . *within* our tradition." To do this we must engage in human dialogue, a dialogue "which combines collectivity with individual responsibility."[14] But if this is the best we can do, one might naturally conclude that the hope of doing any better (i.e., discovering some overarching, objective truth) no longer makes sense. Maybe we should turn away from this goal in philosophy and concentrate merely on the dialogue of humankind. The concepts of objective truth as opposed to subjective truth simply serve no purpose. Within the realm of empirical knowledge, the appearance/reality distinction ought to be rejected. Once again, by denying these distinctions we effectively render moot the skeptic's arguments.

Essentially the post-analytic program in philosophy rests on the denial of the traditional dichotomies—objective/subjective, fact/value, reality/ appearance—that give rise to skepticism. The denial of these dichotomies can, of course, take one of two forms. On the one hand, the very ideas of objective truth, the real world, etc., can be viewed as without merit and rejected. Thus far my emphasis has been on this rejection of an *objective* realm. However, there is another form that the denial of these dichotomies can take. The idea that there is such a thing as a *subjective* realm, a realm composed of mental representations or appearances which does not directly access the external world, can also be denied. In either case, the alleged gap between our observations (how we are appeared to) and the objects which make up the real world is closed—or alleged to have never really existed—with the result that skepticism is no longer seen as a threat to our knowledge. These different positions can be illustrated in the following *aporia*:

(1) The traditional dichotomies that concern epistemologists (objective/ subjective, fact/value, reality/appearance) are false dichotomies.
(2) There exists a real, mind-independent, external world.
(3) We (our minds) do not have direct access to this real, mind-independent, external world.

Rejecting 2 (while accepting 1 and 3) is to deny the objective realm; rejecting 3 (while accepting 1 and 2) is to deny the subjective realm. I will examine the merits of both these views with the aim of demonstrating where they are mistaken. I begin with Donald Davidson and the latter claim: a rejection of the subjective realm.

Davidson and "The Myth of the Subjective"[15]

Davidson, like Putnam and Quine, views the objective/subjective distinction as spurious. According to him, this dichotomy collapses once we recognize the mythical nature of what we have been calling the subjective and rid ourselves of it. The view that the subjective realm (i.e., the deliverances of our senses) is to serve as some sort of foundation for objective empirical knowledge is wrong. Empirical knowledge needs no such foundation. The relationship between the mind and nature is not the kind of relationship envisioned by Descartes. The mind is not isolated and separate from the rest of nature but *directly connected* with nature. Once we recognize this, the Cartesian doubts that make up the skeptic's stock in trade will no longer be relevant. Davidson draws heavily from Quine's program of "naturalized epistemology" in making his claims, so perhaps a brief examination of Quine's arguments in his essay "Epistemology Naturalized" will help make Davidson's position more clear.[16]

As we saw earlier in this chapter, Quine makes the point that there is no objective, value-free perspective from which we can view the world. Our *judgments* about the nature of the external world are always embedded in some sort of theory concerning values. As such, knowledge of the world as a value-free, mind-independent entity is forever beyond our reach. What we are to make of this unhappy conclusion (unhappy for traditional epistemologists) is the subject of "Epistemology Naturalized."

Quine begins by dividing the project of epistemology into two parts: "a theory of concepts, or meaning, and a theory of doctrine, or truth." The first part involves "explaining the notion of body in sensory terms," while the second part involves justifying our knowledge of truths of nature in sensory terms."[17] According to Quine, philosophers have made some progress, although not complete, on the conceptual side of this project. He points to Rudolf Carnap's *Der logische Aufbau der Welt* as the most successful attempt to translate all sentences about the world into sensory terms, logic, and set theory. But, as Quine goes on to assert, "If Carnap had successfully carried out such a construction though, how could he have told whether it was the right one?"[18] Addressing the conceptual side of the project still left the doctrinal side in no better a position vis-à-vis the skeptic than it has been since the time of Hume. As long as the translation worked, and there are many possible translations that could work, the question of rightness or truth never really arises. "The question [is this the *right* construction?] would have no point."[19] And when we raise the doctrinal questions of justification and truth, we find ourselves in the now all too familiar skeptical predicament. As Hume so clearly showed, a fully adequate theory of epistemic justification for empirical knowledge cannot be derived, either deductively or inductively, from observation alone. In Quine's words, "The Humean predicament is the human predicament."[20]

If we accept Quine's arguments to this point, and I believe they are correct, the natural question is why even bother with the conceptual side of the epistemic project? If the doctrinal issues of truth and justification are not addressed by conceptual programs like Carnap's,

> why all this creative reconstruction, all this make believe? The stimulation of sensory receptors is all the evidence anyone has to go on, ultimately, in arriving at his picture of the world. Why not just see how this reconstruction really proceeds? *Why not settle for psychology?*[21] (My emphasis.)

And this is exactly what Quine proposes: to replace traditional epistemology with psychology. In doing so we are left with a *naturalized* epistemology which will deal with questions that really matter to us.

> Epistemology, or something like it, simply falls into place as a chapter of psychology and hence of natural science. It studies a natural phenomenon, viz., a physical human subject. This human subject is accorded a certain experimentally controlled input—certain patterns of irradiation in assorted frequencies, for instance—and in the fullness of time the subject delivers as output a description of the three-dimensional world and its history. The relation between the meagre input and the torrential output is a relation we are prompted to study for somewhat the same reasons that always prompted epistemology; namely, in order to see how evidence relates to theory, and in what ways one's theory of nature transcends any available evidence.[22]

No longer should philosophers engage themselves in *normative* issues involving epistemic justification (projects of this sort are bound to fail), but rather should concentrate their endeavors on the *descriptive* science of cognition, a natural science which falls under the heading of psychology. As Quine describes the change:

> The old epistemology endeavored to contain, in a sense, natural science; it would construct it somehow from sense data. Epistemology in its new setting, conversely, is contained in natural science, as a chapter of psychology.[23]

Davidson recognizes the full import of Quine's program of naturalized epistemology and develops more explicitly its antiskeptical consequences. He begins with what he calls the scheme-content dichotomy (analogous to Quine's conceptual-doctrinal dichotomy). The traditional view is that the mind organizes and interprets experience into objects, events, etc. The concepts used to organize our experiences make up a conceptual scheme. The content side of the dichotomy consists of the things that make up our experiences: sense data, appearances, impressions, etc. The skeptical problem arises when we consider that there is an infinite number of ways a conceptual scheme may organize the data of experience. Some of these schemes may differ radically from our own, even to the point of being incommensurable. How might we determine the correctness of one scheme versus another? There seems to be no neutral position from which we can observe and compare all these various schemes, so the question of correctness of scheme seems without answer. (This was Quine's point in his discussion of Carnap's project of concept construction in *Der logische Aufbau der Welt*.)

For Davidson, this calls into question the very possibility that there are conceptual schemes separate from the contents of our experiences, especially radically different or incommensurable conceptual schemes. In his article, "On the Very Idea of a Conceptual Scheme," he argues as follows. A conceptual scheme, in that it involves interpretation, requires language. Now if two different schemes were radically different, truly incommensurable in the way envisioned by say Thomas Kuhn, then there would be no translation possible between schemes. And if this is the case, how could we ever determine if a conceptual scheme is radically different from our own? It would not be possible, says Davidson. Based on this conclusion, Davidson denies the existence of radically different conceptual schemes. There is more intersubject agreement among peoples and cultures which embrace allegedly different conceptual schemes than most philosophers seem ready to admit. In general, given our common sensory apparatus, we all share roughly the same conceptual scheme.

Of course, if we accept this conclusion, then it seems natural to deny altogether the existence of the subjective, at least insofar as the subjective is to be considered somehow irrevocably divorced from the natural world. As Davidson puts it,

> the idea that there is a basic division between uninterpreted experience and an organizing conceptual scheme [the subjective mind and the objective external world] is a deep mistake, born of the essentially incoherent picture of the mind as a passive but critical spectator of an inner show.[24]

Once we give up this division and accept that the contents of our mind (sense data, appearances, impressions, etc.) can be identified by their causal relations with objects in the world, the problem of skepticism is eliminated. The gap between appearance and reality disappears. The mind is not somehow separate from nature, but interacts with and is a part of nature. The proper project for epistemology is to study this interaction as a natural phenomena without appeal to so called "objects of thought." Epistemologists need to take seriously Quine's call for a "naturalized epistemology" as a chapter in psychology.

The effect of Davidson's and Quine's arguments on the skeptical position should be obvious. Once we see the mind and its alleged contents as merely a part of nature rather than somehow isolated and insulated from it, the problems of skepticism no longer threaten. In fact, we cannot even formulate the problem.

Against Antisubjectivism

The arguments I have attributed to Davidson, Putnam, and Quine can be generally described as antisubjectivist arguments.[25] And while these arguments do eliminate the problem of epistemic skepticism, I believe they do so only by wrongly distorting the project of traditional epistemology. I see two main problems with this antisubjective approach.

The first problem is most clearly seen in Davidson's arguments. Essentially he is offering a transcendental argument which takes as its starting point the possibility of thought. Given that thought is possible, he concludes that skepticism cannot be true. He reaches this result because he views language as a kind of limit on rationality and thought.[26] If skepticism, with its talk of radically different conceptual schemes, were true, then communication between us, which necessarily requires language and some intersubject agreement, would not be possible. And if we cannot communicate and translate between conceptual schemes, then the very idea of language is no longer a coherent concept. But without language to give our thoughts content, thought is no longer possible. As Davidson puts it, "the very possibility of thought demands shared standards of truth and objectivity."[27] Thoughts cannot be purely subjective in the way the skeptic imagines. Therefore, since we are able to entertain thoughts, to include even the thought that skepticism might be true, skepticism *cannot* be true.[28]

Where this argument seems to go wrong is in its presumption concerning the relationship between thought and language. While it does seem true that some language (however basic and primitive) is necessary to get thought, at least reflective thought, started, it also seems true that our thoughts can go beyond our ability to communicate them. In short, our thoughts are far richer than our language, however broadly one might construe the concept of language. Language and communication require "shared standards of truth and objectivity," but thought does not. And although this is a very difficult claim to demonstrate, I think we can see indications of its truth in a number of examples.

Quine's observation concerning the "meagre input" that comes to us via our senses and the "torrential output" of concepts that makes up our theory of nature is one such example. Contrary to Quine, this picture of concept formation is not the result of our world description somehow transcending nature. The "input" is only "meagre" from a quantitative point of view. Qualitatively it is extremely rich—far too rich for our language to handle. For this reason our description results in a "torrential output" in a feeble attempt to capture the full richness of our sense impressions.

Now the failure of our language to handle the input from our senses may be the result of one of two possibilities. The failure may lie with our language, and in time this problem may be overcome as we increasingly enrich that language. If this is the case, my arguments leave Davidson's position intact. Translation between conceptual schemes is still in principle always possible, and therefore, the possibility of incommensurable schemes, and the subjective realm this possibility entails, is still blocked. However, if the failure of language is the result of something fundamentally deeper than a mere need to enrich our language, than the myth of the subjective seems resurrected. Davidson recognizes this possibility. "At this point one can imagine a proposal to the effect that there are *inexpressible phenomenal criteria* to which the publicly expressible criteria can be reduced" (my emphasis). But he quickly adds, "it is to be hoped that memories of past failures of such reductionist fantasies will serve to suppress the thought that the proposal could be carried out."[29]

My own view is that there are "inexpressible phenomenal criteria," and the failure of "reductionist fantasies" is—contrary to Davidson—an epistemic failure rather than a metaphysical failure. In other words, the inexpressibility of the phenomenal criteria is not an indication that these criteria do not exist. Rather, it illustrates once again that the "Humean predicament is the human predicament," and we are perforce limited by our unique and private subjective perspective of the world. The subjective realm is not a myth.

This leads to a second objection to antisubjectivism and the naturalized epistemology the antisubjectivist advocates. I have no doubt that the kinds of inquiries favored by Davidson, Putnam, Quine, and others—inquiries in the fields of cognitive science and psychology—will prove very fruitful and important. However, it is a mistake to presume that such inquiries should and will replace epistemology. That it is a mistake can seen if we go back to some of the arguments I offered against externalist, nondoxastic theories in chapter 5. Although they are not exactly the same, there is a close analogy between naturalized epistemology and these externalist theories.[30] In both theories the focus is on that which we would normally consider outside or external to the putative knower. And while this is a legitimate realm of inquiry, it does not really touch on the issue of epistemic justification in a way that addresses the skeptical concerns of the individual knower.

One of the crucial issues for any theory of knowledge is first-person belief justification. We don't just want to know how knowledge is possible, but we also want to know what knowledge is *actual for me*. Epistemic justification is not merely a set of facts to be described by psychologists in terms of some connection, causal or otherwise, between ourselves and the external world. While these connections may play an important role in any theory of epistemic justification, first-person epistemic justification necessarily involves some sort of first-person judgment, e.g., am *I* now connected with the external world in the requisite manner to confer justification on my belief that there is a river outside of my window, and *how* do *I* know I am so connected? It is this first-person aspect of belief justification that naturalized epistemology ignores.

Why is this first-person aspect of epistemic justification ignored? The answer seems to be that by addressing it, we open up the possibility that skepticism is the correct theory. But that is the very possibility that a theory of knowledge is intended to defeat (or at least mitigate). We cannot defeat skepticism by refusing to entertain its possibility, yet that is what the proponents of naturalized epistemology seem to be doing. Cognitive science and psychology can make important contributions in the field of epistemology, but they offer only a partial account human knowledge. Natural science, far from subsuming traditional epistemology, is properly seen as contained in that philosophical tradition.

So much for the antisubjectivist move of post-analytic philosophy. In the next chapter I will look at the other way in which post-analytical philosophers have attempted to deny the objective/subjective dichotomy, viz., by rejecting the objective realm.

Notes

1. Immanuel Kant, *Prolegomena to Any Future Metaphysics*, trans. Lewis White Beck (Indianapolis: Bobbs-Merrill, 1950.), 61–62.
2. Ludwig Wittgenstein, *Philosophical Investigations*, 3rd ed., trans. G. E. M. Anscombe (New York: Macmillan Publishing Co., 1958), pt. 1, para. 43.
3. Wittgenstein, *Philosophical Investigations*, pt. 1, para. 98.
4. Wittgenstein, *Philosophical Investigations*, pt. 1, para. 107.
5. Wittgenstein, *Philosophical Investigations*, pt. 1, para. 241.
6. Wittgenstein, *Philosophical Investigations*, pt. 1, para. 242.
7. This seems to agree with Stanley Cavell's general view of Wittgenstein's *Investigations* in his book *The Claim of Reason* (Oxford: Oxford University Press, 1979); see especially chapters I and II.
8. Willard V. O. Quine, *Ontological Relativity and Other Essays* (New York: Columbia University Press, 1969), 26–68.
9. Quine makes a similar claim in discussing the analytic-synthetic distinction in "Two Dogmas of Empiricism" (*From A Logical Point of View* [Cambridge: Harvard University Press, 1964], 20–46).
10. Hilary Putnam, *Reason, Truth, and History* (Cambridge: Cambridge University Press, 1981), especially chapter 6 and 9.
11. Putnam, *Reason, Truth, and History*, 201.
12. This seems true even in the allegedly objective and value-free realm of the physical sciences as Thomas Kuhn has shown in *The Structure of Scientific Revolution* (2nd. ed., enlarged [Chicago: University of Chicago Press, 1970]); see especially chapter X.
13. Putnam, *Reason, Truth, and History*, 215.
14. Putnam, *Reason, Truth, and History*, 216.
15. In discussing Donald Davidson's position I will be drawing on the following two articles: "On the Very Idea of a Conceptual Scheme" (in *Post-Analytic Philosophy*, ed. John Rajchman and Cornell West [New York: Columbia University Press, 1985], 129–43) and "The Myth of the Subjective" (in *Relativism: Interpretation and Confrontation*, ed. Michael Krausz [Notre Dame, Ind.: University of Notre Dame Press, 1989], 159–72).
16. Quine, *Ontological Relativity and Other Essays*, 69–90.
17. Quine, *Ontological Relativity and Other Essays*, 71.
18. Quine, *Ontological Relativity and Other Essays*, 75.
19. Ibid.
20. Quine, *Ontological Relativity and Other Essays*, 72.
21. Quine, *Ontological Relativity and Other Essays*, 75.
22. Quine, *Ontological Relativity and Other Essays*, 82–83.
23. Quine, *Ontological Relativity and Other Essays*, 83.
24. Davidson, "The Myth of the Subjective," 171.
25. Davidson has coined this term to characterize his position. See "The Myth of the Subjective," 167.
26. Putnam essentially makes the same point in chapter 9 of *Reason, Truth, and History*. See especially 214–16.
27. Davidson, "The Myth of the Subjective," 171.
28. This argument is very much like Putnam's argument concerning the self-refuting nature of the skeptic's "brains in a vat" possibility. See *Reason, Truth, and History*, chapter 1.

29. Davidson, "The Myth of the Subjective," 170.

30. Alvin Plantinga, for one, is very explicit on this point and claims that his theory of proper function is very much a naturalistic one. See his *Warrant and Proper Function* (New York: Oxford University Press, 1993), 45–46.

Chapter Eight

Post-Analytical Solutions to Skepticism, Part II

As may be recalled, we started our discussion of Davidson's antisubjectivism with the following *aporia*:

(1) The traditional dichotomies that concern epistemologists (objective/subjective, fact/value, reality/appearance) are false dichotomies.
(2) There exists a real, mind-independent, external world.
(3) We (our minds) do not have direct access to this real, mind-independent, external world.

Davidson rejects 3, but others have resolved this *aporia* by rejecting 2 and embracing 1 and 3. Richard Rorty's arguments in *Philosophy and the Mirror of Nature* and *Contingency, Irony, and Solidarity* are examples of this latter line of argumentation. I select Rorty to represent this post-analytic position for several reasons. First, his presentation is exceptionally clear and thus very accessible. Second, his arguments are presently at the center of a great deal of philosophical interest.

Rorty and the Mirror of Nature

Rorty's main contention is that the focus of philosophy stands in need of change. The traditional focus of philosophy as rational inquiry with the discovery of truth as its goal is misguided (and he cites many of the skeptical arguments I summarized in my last chapter in support of this thesis). The proper focus should not be the elusive objective truth postulated by the skeptic but consensus and victory in argument. We should view truth as "a matter of conversation between persons, rather than a matter of interaction with nonhuman reality."[1] Instead of aiming at objectivity, Rorty suggests "solidarity" as a better goal. Solidarity, unlike objective truth, is something that is made, not discovered. Our goal should be to expand solidarity or consensus among people rather than expand truth. Such a view of philosophy will free us to the possibility of moral progress by giving us a better understanding of alternate points of view.[2]

The reason we have not been able to make such a move in philosophy (from objectivity to solidarity) is because philosophy, particularly epistemology, has been dominated by the image of the "Mirror of Nature," according to Rorty. For too long we have conceived of knowledge as representations in this Mirror. As such, our goal has been to discover a foundation for knowledge consisting of a "special privileged class of representations so compelling that their accuracy cannot be doubted."[3] Traditional philosophy has always depended on finding such a privileged perspective, a neutral framework of inquiry. But, as Quine's arguments make clear, there is no such privileged class of representations or neutral framework available to us. Therefore we would be better to drop the notion of philosophy as a search for such a framework and turn to a new conception of philosophy and knowledge. We need to "substitute Freedom for truth as the goal of thinking and of social progress."[4]

In making this substitution, the philosopher will have to take on a new role. She must not think of herself as a high priestess of knowledge but must take the poet as her role model.[5] Instead of focusing on "how things really are" we would be better off if our focus was what Rorty calls *edification.*

> The attempt to edify (ourselves or others) may consist in the hermeneutical activity of making connections between our own culture and some exotic culture or historical period, or between our own discipline and another discipline which seems to pursue incommensurable aims in an incommensurable vocabulary. But it may instead consist in the "poetic" activity of thinking up such new aims, new words, or new disciplines, followed by . . . the attempt to reinterpret our familiar surroundings in the unfamiliar terms of our new inventions.[6]

Rather than searching for an ideal language, a privileged perspective, a neutral framework, we should remain open to new vocabularies, new perspectives, new models, in much the way the poet is open to new creative processes. Philosophers can do this by embracing a mode of inquiry known as *hermeneutics.*

Hermeneutics, as that branch of knowledge involving the interpretation of texts, has a long history. Its antecedents are found in the Reformation dispute between the Catholic Church and Martin Luther involving the interpretation of the spiritual truth found in the Bible. The Church's position after the Council of

Trent was that correct interpretation of the scriptures involved discerning the author's intent. Such discernment, of necessity, relied on the tradition of the Church as a bridge back to the author's intent. Luther disagreed. For him scripture was to be understood from the text alone, with, of course, the aid of inspiration. The author's original intent was something in the past; correct interpretation of scriptural truth was a question of finding the intention embodied in the text itself.[7] From the issue of spiritual truth as embodied in the Bible, hermeneutics as a discipline eventually began to concern itself with the interpretation of all texts and all truths. It is at this point that philosophy, and epistemology in particular, began to take an interest in hermeneutical interpretation.

Rorty's view of the philosopher as poet and philosophy as a quest for solidarity owes much to the hermeneutical philosophy of Hans-Georg Gadamer. Gadamer's view of philosophy as a hermeneutical enterprise is largely contained in his book *Truth and Method*.[8] Following in the tradition of Martin Heidegger, Gadamer sees hermeneutics as a kind of resolution of the problems of epistemology. Gadamer's thesis concerns the "openness of the text" or the undecidability of translation. He agrees with Luther that the *understanding* of a text only comes when the reader applies the text to himself, but he rejects Luther's idea that the text has a unique, correct *interpretation. Understanding* and *interpretation* are not independent of each other. All understanding involves interpretation and vice-versa.[9] This interdependence of understanding and interpretation is what Gadamer calls the *hermeneutical circle of understanding*. As he puts it:

> The anticipation of meaning [understanding], in which the whole is projected, is brought to explicit comprehension in that the parts, determined by the whole, determine their whole as well.[10] (My brackets.)

Applying the hermeneutical circle to epistemology, we see that there can be no such thing as an objective understanding of the external world. All our understanding of the world involves interpretation, which in turn involves some understanding of the world. That is why we need to be more open and poetlike in our philosophical endeavors. Instead of searching for that one perspective, that one method which will give us objective knowledge, we need to engage in hermeneutical conversation which leaves open the possibility of new and varied perspectives.

In embracing this new, hermeneutical role for philosophy, we will also be forced to embrace a new concept of mankind. Traditional philosophy, from the time of Plato and Aristotle to the present, has always conceived of man as having a metaphysically significant nature, an essence. Mankind is different from the other animals and objects in the universe in that we have this special essence, namely, to discover essences.[11] However, such a conception of mankind is a form of self-deception and is responsible for many of the dilemmas faced by philosophy. If we are, by nature, discoverers of essences, then there must be essences to discover, i.e., a unique referent for such terms as the Truth, the Real, the Good. But this creates a dilemma for the philosopher. He must, on the one hand,

> attempt to find criteria for picking out these unique referents, whereas, on the other hand, the only hints he has about what these criteria could be are provided by current practice (by, e.g., the best moral and scientific thought of the day). Philosophers thus condemn themselves to a Sisyphean task.[12]

We break free of this dilemma once we realize the self-defeating nature of our conception of humankind (something hermeneutics helps us to realize) and adopt a "wholehearted behaviorism, naturalism, and physicalism" in which we are no different from "inkwells or atoms."[13]

All these changes in our way of viewing ourselves and our understanding of the world around us can be viewed as a change from *systematic* to *edifying* philosophy, according to Rorty. He draws the distinction in the following manner:

> Great systematic philosophers are constructive and offer arguments. Great edifying philosophers are reactive and offer satires, parodies, aphorisms. They know their work loses its point when the period they were reacting against is over. They are *intentionally* peripheral. Great systematic philosophers, like great scientists, build for eternity. Great edifying philosophers destroy for the sake of their own generation. Systematic philosophers want to put their subject on the secure path of science. Edifying philosophers want to keep space open for the sense of wonder which poets can sometimes cause—wonder that there is something new under the sun, something which is *not* an accurate representation of what was already there, something which (at least for the moment) cannot be explained and can barely be described.[14]

And what is the payoff we realize in adopting these changes? What is the point of a philosophy that is merely reactive? "The point of edifying philosophy is to keep the conversation going rather than to find objective truth."[15] The great fear of edifying philosophy is that the conversation of mankind may one day end. If we postulate an objectively true or false answer to every question we deny "the possibility of something new under the sun, of human life as poetic rather than merely contemplative."[16] The very possibility that we may someday have all the answers to all the questions acts as a constraint on "free and leisured conversation." The remedy, according to Rorty, is to

> see knowing not as having an essence, to be described by scientists or philosophers, but rather a right, by current standards, to believe, then we are well on our way to seeing *conversation* as the ultimate context within which knowledge is to be understood.[17]

By way of summary, let me briefly spell out the changes Rorty is recommending as we move from *systematic philosophy* to *edifying philosophy*.

Essentially he is recommending a change in vocabulary, a change in the way we describe our situation. I outline these changes below:

From	To
Systematic Philosophy	→ Edifying Philosophy
Objectivity	→ Solidarity
Truth	→ Freedom
Philosopher as Priestess	→ Philosopher as Poet
Man as Metaphysically Significant	→ Man as a Naturalistic, Physical Being
Knowledge as Grasping the Truth	→ Knowledge as Conversation

Skeptical Objections to Post-Analytic Philosophy

How does traditional philosophy respond to the recommendations of edifying philosophy? In particular, what is skepticism's rejoinder to Rorty? It seems that the skeptic's objections can be classified into two main sorts. On the one hand there are objections which are internal to Rorty's system of edifying philosophy. That is, they accept the validity of the hermeneutical response to skepticism but question whether such a response will really accomplish what it is meant to accomplish. On the other hand there are objections which may be raised external to the edifying system of philosophy. These objections question the very need for the hermeneutical posture recommended by Rorty.

Turning first to internal objections, the changes in vocabulary that Rorty recommends are somehow suppose to be *better* than the vocabulary of traditional, systematic philosophy, and yet it is difficult to ascertain how it is that the new vocabulary is better. What is the standard against which we are to measure the new vocabulary as *better*? It is *better* relative to what? Part of the problem lies in what Rorty calls the paradox of the edifying philosopher. As a *philosopher*, the edifying philosopher is seen as presenting arguments. But as an edifying philosopher, he sees himself more in the role of a poet. As a poet, he is merely presenting an alternate vocabulary without presenting an argument for or against that vocabulary. As Rorty puts it, the edifying philosopher is in the awkward position of having "to decry the very notion of having a view, while avoiding having a view about having views."[18]

While this is an awkward position for the edifying philosopher, Rorty does not see it as impossible. Citing Wittgenstein and Heidegger as examples, he makes the point that the edifying philosopher "might just be *saying something*— participating in a conversation rather than contributing to an inquiry."[19] But this seems altogether too facile a response. Surely the conversation has a point. Even if the edifying philosopher's contribution to the conversation of philosophy consists only in ejaculations which are neither true or false (a sort of epistemological emotivism), surely these ejaculations are being offered to influence our attitudes. They are offering us some sort of *recommendation*, to use a favorite term of Rorty's. In view of this commendatory feature of the edifying philosopher's conversation, he must have *reasons* for his recommended changes. A recommendation without reasons to back it up (even if the only reason is only that we will be better off for adopting this change) is no recommendation at all. It is of no real value.

However, here it might be objected that I am not taking the edifying philosopher's project at its face value. The value of the conversation does not consist in any commendatory nature we might perceive it to have, rather the value is merely the conversation itself. The value of edifying philosophy lies in its ability to keep the conversation going. But even this claim (if I may be so bold as to label it a claim) seems problematic. Edifying philosophy is merely "reactive" in nature. The edifying philosopher is in the business of destroying systems, not building them up. Yet, if he is engaged in destruction, there must be something (call it systematic philosophy) to destroy. *Reaction* can only occur against the backdrop of *action*. If all of philosophy were to subscribe to the hermeneutical project of reaction, what direction could the conversation take? In the end, it seems, the conversation must end (or perhaps endlessly babble on, destroying that which is already destroyed). In either case, edifying philosophy seems to be in no better position than traditional philosophy (and maybe worse) to insure the continuation of the philosophical conversation of mankind. In fact (as I will argue in the next chapter), skepticism, the kind of skepticism I am advocating, is in a much better position to insure the continuation of the dialogue begun by Plato and the other Greek philosophers. Without the "Sisyphean" work of systematic philosophy, there is nothing to motivate the hermeneutical dialogue of Rorty, Gadamer, and others. A dialogue which is merely reactive in nature and devoid of constructive content is likely to realize the great fear of edifying philosophy: the end of conversation.

There is one final objection I would like to make, internal to the hermeneutical project, before moving on to other, more external objections. This objection concerns the post-analytical view of *objective truth*. Simply put, their view is that there is no such thing. What is the basis for their conclusion? Essentially it is the failure of epistemology to discover this truth that leads them to suppose that it does not exist. They cite the work of philosophers such as Wittgenstein, Kuhn, Quine, and Putnam to demonstrate that objective truth is not to be found in language, science, or any other allegedly neutral framework or foundation. In that philosophy has been working to no avail at this project of discovering the objective truth for over 2,000 years, perhaps it is time to consider the possibility that there is no such truth waiting to be discovered.

While I will admit that such a view of truth is possible, the basis edifying philosophy cites for holding such a view is, at best, problematic. The arguments they cite are epistemic arguments. They are arguments that question our ability to *know* the truth, arguments that are in harmony with the skeptic's position (and best read as skeptical arguments in my opinion). There is no necessary connection between these *epistemic* arguments and the *ontological* claim that there is no objective truth. The epistemic arguments may lay down some sort of presumptive case for the post-analytic, antirealist view of truth, but such a presumptive case seems no stronger than the presumptive case I made for objective truth and realism in chapter 3. Furthermore, as I pointed out then, Rorty's view of objective truth is question begging in the extreme vis-à-vis the skeptical argument. What his position amounts to is a claim that our knowledge of the *real truth* is immune to skeptical doubts because there is no such thing as the *real truth*.

Additionally, abandoning the concept of objective truth and the real world seems to have disastrous consequences for philosophical inquiry. I will have more to say on this subject in the next chapter, but for know let me at least make this point. If the continuation of the conversation of mankind is as important a goal as Rorty has made it out to be, I can see no better way to motivate that conversation than by a close examination of our alleged knowledge of the truth (objectively understood) and how that knowledge is subject to skeptical doubts.

This last point leads us naturally into a discussion of the very value of the hermeneutical project and my external objections. The focus of philosophical inquiry, particularly in the discipline of epistemology, has generally been on the individual. How is it that the putative knower knows that *p*? How do *I* come to have knowledge of the external world? What justifies my claim to know *p*. It is questions such as these that have motivated and occupied epistemologists. Rorty, however, gives us a different focus. His concern is with the community at large and the development of solidarity and consensus within the community. There is nothing wrong in principle with this difference in focus; the mistake is in trying to apply this community focus to the concerns of the individual inquirer.[20]

The concerns and motivations of the community can be, and often are, at odds with those of the individual. The parking regulations at my college may not fit my individual needs as well as I would like, but in order that everyone in the college community (including myself) attain some minimum satisfaction of their need to find a parking space, I may have to forego some of my desires, give up the belief that my need to park is somehow special or privileged. Successful community life depends on this kind of cooperation and consensus, sometimes at the expense of individual freedoms and desires. But the attainment of community consensus is not what motivates individual philosophical inquiry. For example, it is really not important that everyone agree with my assessment of my epistemic status. Even if I could come up with a position in epistemology that satisfies everyone, my inquiry into the nature of knowledge would not end unless I believed my position to be *true*, i.e., the objectively correct theory. Consensus is just not enough. I am interested in discovering the truth—not agreement. As Nicholas Rescher points out, "In philosophy we should neither expect our position to be the focus of a consensus nor be discouraged when it fails to be so."[21] For what motivates and directs community conversation and practice, namely, the need for solidarity and consensus, is not a factor in individual philosophical inquiry. To try and impose the framework of the former on the latter is to make a kind of category mistake—and this is just what Rorty seems to do.

Rorty's category mistake is all the more pernicious when we realize the cost incurred by his change in focus and vocabulary. If we view the project of traditional philosophy as rational inquiry aimed at discovering universal, objective truths (a view of traditional philosophy that Rorty would agree with, although he finds such a inquiry as without merit), it is a view that we give up with great difficulty—despite Rorty's recommendations. Such a view of philosophical inquiry seems a necessary part of our intellectual life. As skepticism makes all too clear to us, we are creatures of finite intellect; our memories can only store so much raw data; we do not enjoy a God's-eye view of the universe. In order to expand our view of the world beyond mere bits of data, we necessarily make use of inductive generalizations, draw inferences which go beyond the evidence at hand, in short, *do the best we can* despite the narrowness of our perspective and the uncertainty of our claims.

Even though the fortress of skepticism appears theoretically unassailable, we still must live out our lives and make our way in the world. We can do so in one of two ways. We can either follow in the footsteps of post-analytical philosophy and deny the very existence of a unifying, godlike perspective, wherein the objective truth resides, or we can postulate the existence of such a objective, all-encompassing viewpoint—even if it is beyond our ability to fully grasp. The post-analytic turn seems fraught with many shortcomings and dangers. Beyond a vague quest for consensus, there is nothing to motivate our dialogue. Our inquiries seem condemned to chaos and confusion. Then, once we reach a consensus, what is the point of further dialogue. In the 1930s, the German people reached a fairly complete consensus on the desirability of a National Socialist State. Is this the kind of consensus that is to be countenanced by edifying philosophy? Is there any real basis upon which the edifying philosopher can reject such a conversation and consensus as false and wrong?

Better to postulate the existence of an objective truth, an absolute Good, to motivate and guide (however loosely and imperfectly) our philosophical inquiries. Even if the task of discovering these truths is theoretically impossible ("Sisyphean," to use Rorty's description), there seems something good and noble in engaging in the quest. Camus, in his essay "The Myth of Sisyphus," brings the nobleness of this quest into sharp focus. Despite the apparent absurdity and futility of the task, Sisyphus always returns to the bottom of the hill to roll his rock up the mountain. He is condemned to this life, much like we are "condemned" to search the heights of our intellect for a truth that we can never fully grasp. But, at the end of the essay Camus is led to conclude, "The struggle itself towards the heights is enough to fill a man's heart. One must imagine

Sisyphus happy."[22] In much the same way, I imagine the traditional philosopher as happy.

Now I do not intend to prescribe the kind of existential view toward life and philosophy that Camus argues for. For one thing, I see more usefulness and less absurdity in our epistemic task than Camus allows. But I do think there is some truth in what he says. We cannot seem to give up our struggle to discover some rational truth or meaning to our lives. What else can explain our continued obsession for over 2,000 years with discovering the truth. That is why Sisyphus continues to roll the rock up the hill and is happy doing so. He cannot stop himself from engaging in the task. It is a part of living and making our way in the world.[23] No change in vocabulary, no change in focus, is going to change this one fact. However futile we perceive the search, we are unable to give it up.

Of course Rorty would explain this obsession with the truth as a case of self-deception. We mistakenly view ourselves as possessing some metaphysically significant essence, a "Glassy Essence" as he sometimes calls it, which compels us to engage in this task. He may be right, but I for one am unable to give up this alleged self-deception. The history of philosophical inquiry has been largely motivated by such a "mistaken" view. If Rorty is searching for consensus and solidarity, what better place to find it than in the more than 2,000 years of consensus within the philosophical community of mankind?

Conclusion

What then are we to make of Rorty, Davidson, and their post-analytical colleagues? It seems that they have got only half the story right—the skeptical, epistemic half. They, and most of the philosophers that they trace their lineage from (Heidegger, Wittgenstein, Kuhn, Quine, Gadamer, etc.) are best viewed, in my opinion, as skeptical philosophers. However, the ontological conclusion that they draw from their skepticism—that there is no subjective realm somehow separate from the external world or that there is no objective realm to be discovered—is wrong. Better to live with skepticism than with a rejection of the existence of either the subjective realm or the objective truth. Rejecting either horn of the subjective-objective dilemma does not resolve or dissolve the skeptic's arguments; it merely ignores them. I, for one, would rather embrace the skeptic's arguments than pretend they do not exist. That leads us to some final questions. How can we embrace and live with skepticism? Why is skepticism a better alternative than hermeneutical posturing? These questions and others concerning the value of skepticism are the subject of my next chapter.

Notes

1. Richard Rorty, *Philosophy and the Mirror of Nature* (Princeton: Princeton University Press, 1979), 156.

2. Rorty, *Contingency, Irony, and Solidarity* (Cambridge: Cambridge University Press, 1989), 196–98.

3. Rorty, *Philosophy and the Mirror of Nature*, 163.

4. Rorty, *Contingency, Irony, and Solidarity*, xiii.

5. Rorty, *Contingency, Irony, and Solidarity*, 26.

6. Rorty, *Philosophy and the Mirror of Nature*, 360.

7. See *Hermeneutics Versus Science? Three German Views*, ed. John M. Connolly and Thomas Keutner (Notre Dame, Ind.: University of Notre Dame Press, 1988), 1–67, for more on the historical background to hermeneutics.

8. Hans-Georg Gadamer, *Truth and Method*, trans. G. Barden and J. Cummings (New York: Crossroad, 1988).

9. Gadamer, *Truth and Method*, 351–66.

10. Gadamer, "On the Circle of Understanding" in *Hermeneutics Versus Science? Three German Views* (Notre Dame, Ind.: University of Notre Dame Press, 1988), 68.

11. Rorty, *Philosophy and the Mirror of Nature*, 357.

12. Rorty, *Philosophy and the Mirror of Nature*, 374. This is essentially a restatement of Chisholm's problem of the criterion.

13. Rorty, *Philosophy and the Mirror of Nature*, 373.

14. Rorty, *Philosophy and the Mirror of Nature*, 369–70.

15. Rorty, *Philosophy and the Mirror of Nature*, 377.

16. Rorty, *Philosophy and the Mirror of Nature*, 389.

17. Ibid.

18. Rorty, *Philosophy and the Mirror of Nature*, 371.

19. Ibid.

20. I owe this point to Nicholas Rescher. See his *The Strife of Systems: An Essay on the Grounds and Implications of Philosophical Diversity* (Pittsburgh: University of Pittsburgh Press, 1985), chapter 10, especially 196–99.

21. Rescher, *The Strife of Systems*, 199.

22. Albert Camus, "The Myth of Sisyphus," in *The Myth of Sisyphus and Other Essays* (New York: Vintage Books, 1955), 91.

23. I might add that there are a number of other roles and tasks that we take on in life (husband, wife, parent, friend, to name just a few) that are every bit as Sisyphean (and noble) as the traditional philosopher's role as a searcher for truth, yet we do not give up these roles and tasks simply because we are not and can never be the perfect husband, wife, parent, friend.

Chapter Nine

Theory, Practice, and Skepticism

The arguments of the last eight chapters have put us in a position to ask what I believe is the most important question of this book: what do we make of the apparent success of skepticism? All the theories of knowledge that I have examined thus far have foundered on the issue of truth. With the exception of the post-analytic view of epistemology, the ability of these numerous theories of knowledge to lead us to the truth has been found lacking. Their standards of epistemic justification have all failed the requirement for metajustification that I defended in the second chapter. The post-analytic philosophers skirt this problem of truth-conduciveness as embodied in the requirement for metajustification only by denying the need for the requirement altogether. By rejecting a sharp distinction between appearance and reality, the requirement that our standards of epistemic justification somehow bridge the gap between the two becomes moot.

Now while the post-analytic stance toward skepticism seems clearly wrong (for reasons I've already given in my last chapter), the issues which underlie this view of philosophy do, I think, offer us a clue as to how we might answer the question I posed at the beginning of this chapter. In a sense, the post-analytic program is an attempt to answer this question. Within the context of traditional philosophy they concede the success of skepticism and go on to ask: What does this success portend for traditional philosophy? After all, the point of edifying philosophy is not to provide a *solution* to skepticism, at least not in our normal understanding of a *solution*. Rather, the only point they may be trying to make is that traditional philosophers have a wrong view of the project of epistemology in particular, and of philosophy in general. This view that the traditional conception of philosophy is somehow mistaken is what seems to lie at the heart of many of their claims. Gadamer is especially explicit on this point, and using Aristotle's explication of the intellectual virtues in the *Nichomachean Ethics*, attempts to illustrate the nature of this mistake. Gadamer's use of Aristotle seems especially illuminating. On the one hand I think it further helps explain how the project of post-analytic philosophy manages to go awry. On the other hand, I believe that Aristotle's taxonomy of intellectual virtues provides the clue we need to happily reconcile the project of traditional epistemology with the apparent success of skepticism. However, before discussing Gadamer's use of Aristotle, a brief sketch of Aristotle's taxonomy of intellectual virtues seems in order.

Aristotle's Intellectual Virtues

Aristotle's discussion of virtue is largely found in book six of the *Nichomachean Ethics*. He begins by dividing virtues into two separate classifications: the virtues of the character and the virtues of the intellect.[1] The virtues of the intellect are aimed at attaining the truth, so these are the virtues which will interest us here. These intellectual virtues are further subdivided into scientific and calculative parts.[2] It is this subdivision of intellectual virtues—scientific vs. calculative—that I find most interesting. It offers what I believe is a very important perspective on the value and impact of skepticism on traditional philosophy, as well as on the way we ought to live our lives. In order to capture this perspective we need to first examine Aristotle's own formulation of the division between the scientific and calculative modes of thinking. Then I will explore how Gadamer and Rorty make use of Aristotle's taxonomy of intellectual virtues.

For Aristotle, the scientific aspect of the intellectual virtues concerns itself with the realm of theory. Aristotle classifies three modes of thought which fall under the theoretical realm: *episteme* (scientific knowledge), *nous* (intelligence or intuition), and *sophia* (theoretical wisdom), but it is primarily *episteme* which concerns us here. For Aristotle, *episteme* is knowledge whose object is necessary, universal truth. These truths are eternal truths because, as he puts it, "everything that *is of necessity* in the unqualified sense is eternal." Capable of demonstration, scientific knowledge can be deduced from first principles or universals.[3] It is *episteme* then which Aristotle sees as giving us objective knowledge of the physical world around us, the kind of knowledge natural science strives for.

The calculative or deliberative part of the intellectual virtues are those modes of thought concerned with human activity. According to Aristotle, the knowledge we attain from them is practical in nature rather than theoretical. *Techne* (art or technical skill) is the first of these practical modes of thought. *Techne* is concerned with the reasoned production of artifacts, the kind of skill a builder or a sculptor has. It is a skill that can be learned either through experience or through teaching. However, it is not concerned with action or conduct—what Aristotle calls *praxis*.[4] *Praxis* is the concern of prudence or practical wisdom (*phronesis*). It has as its object the reasoned deliberation and subsequent judgment about what *ought* to be done in a particular case or situation. It requires a degree of self-deliberation and self-knowledge, for the prudent man, says Aristotle, is one who "can envisage what is good for [himself] and for people in general."[5] *Phronesis* is closely connected with *praxis* because *phronesis* has the nature of a command. It presents us with a kind of moral imperative.

This completes Aristotle's classification of intellectual virtues. As can be seen, the main distinction he draws is between theoretical, scientific reasoning on the one hand and practical, moral reasoning on the other hand. I now turn to Gadamer and his use of Aristotle's taxonomy.

Gadamer and Aristotle

One of Gadamer's main concerns is moral knowledge and the practices which are guided by this knowledge. In particular, he sees moral knowledge as being corrupted by modern man's increasing infatuation with science and technology. As a result of this infatuation, the distinction between scientific theory and practical, moral knowledge has been distorted. It is Gadamer's view that modern man, to his detriment, has come to excessively rely on the efficacy of theory over practice. In order to correct the distortion this excessive reliance has caused, Gadamer advocates we return to Aristotle and his views in the *Ethics*. As he puts it:

> . . . the great merit of Aristotle was that he anticipated the impasse of our scientific culture by his description of the structure of practical reason as distinct from theoretical knowledge and technical skill. By philosophical arguments he refuted the claims of professional lawmakers whose function at that time corresponded to the role of the expert in the modern scientific society. . . . Modern society expects him [the scientific expert] to provide a substitute for past moral and political orientations. Consequently, the concept of "*praxis*" which was developed in the last two centuries is an awful deformation of what practice really is. In all debates of the last century practice was understood as the application of science to technical tasks. . . . It degrades practical reason to technical control.[6]

The problem, if I understand Gadamer correctly, is that modern man, lured by the admittedly amazing successes of science and technology, sees these modes of thought as holding the key to resolving the moral problems faced by mankind. This reliance on science and technology over practical wisdom is a mistake and distorts the proper relationship between theory and practice. Within the essentially moral realm of *praxis* he sees a need to reestablish the primacy of practice over theory. A present-day example of the kind of distortion that concerns Gadamer might include the hope that a space-based defense system (the United States' Strategic Defense Initiative) would provide a feasible solution to the nuclear arms race and the terror of nuclear warfare. Other examples might include the hope that new medical technologies, such as genetic engineering and the development of artificial organs, will provide mankind with an ever longer and somehow better life.

Yet, for all the hope that science and technology offers, for every problem that is solved, old problems remain and new ones arise. And interestingly enough, these unresolved problems are often more fundamental and bewildering than the original problems our scientific theories and technologies were meant to address. This is, I take it, Gadamer's point. The Strategic Defense Initiative does not resolve the problems of super-power confrontation that lie at the root of the arms race. Advances in genetic engineering, such as the ability to clone and splice genes, seem prone to abuse and open up very difficult moral issues concerning human nature and what it is to be human. Our scientific and technological ability to prolong life fails to address a number of deeper questions. When is it *right* to prolong a life? Is mere survival, in any form, a desirable goal? What constitutes a quality life? It is as if science and technology too often merely treat symptoms without attacking the root causes that are at the base of these perplexing problems. It might be argued, as Gadamer often seems to, that science and technology, in so far as they introduce new problems and fail to adequately address the fundamental *human* problems of society, are actually problems themselves.

This increasing reliance on technology as a means to solve the very *human* problems we face and must grapple with in our daily lives, has blinded us according to Gadamer. The belief that technical skill and scientific theory (Aristotle's *techne* and *episteme*) can be applied unproblematically to the resolution of the practical concerns of *praxis* is a mistake. Moral knowledge, the kind of knowledge that should guide our *praxis*, cannot be attain through the application of technical solutions (as the examples above are meant to illustrate), but requires a certain kind of self-deliberation. This kind of self-deliberation, and the self-knowledge it produces, is one of the marks of *phronesis*. In the words of Gadamer:

> It is not the case that dependence on moral knowledge, the process of self-deliberation, would be completely done away with by extending technical knowledge. Moral knowledge can never be knowable in advance in the manner of knowledge that can be taught [i.e., scientific and technical knowledge]. The relation between means and ends here is not such that the knowledge of the right means can be made available in advance, and that because the knowledge of the right end is not the mere object of knowledge either. There can be no anterior certainty concerning what the good life is directed towards as a whole. Hence Aristotle's definitions of *phronesis* have a marked uncertainty

about them, in that this knowledge is sometimes related more to the end, and sometimes more to the means to the end.[7]

We need to be sensitive, is Gadamer's claim, to the differences between theoretical, scientific knowledge and practical, moral knowledge. The former cannot substitute for the latter. Admittedly, technological skill combined with scientific theory have brought about solutions to a host of practical problems. In many cases technology has served as a sort of bridge between our theories and their application to the practical problems we face in the world. Our ever-improving technological skill holds out the promise that advances in technology will allow us to apply our theoretical knowledge to practical problems of day-to-day living. This idea of technology as a bridge between theory and practice is what gives technology its great appeal. The hope is that by improving our scientific theory and technology we will eventually be able to resolve most, if not all, the practical, moral problems we face in making our way through this world. However, Gadamer claims this is not a realistic hope and leads us to distort the role and relationship of technology to scientific theory and practical, moral knowledge.

Concerning the efficacy of applying scientific and technological solutions to the practical problems of moral action, Gadamer seems correct to me. The knowledge of scientific theory can have no unproblematic application in practice, especially moral practice. The reason for this is that the theoretical knowledge of science operates within the realm of absolute principles, perfect rationality, and certain data. It is the world of frictionless planes, sharp boundaries, and ideal conditions. Practical knowledge, with its concern for conduct, is interested not only in the theoretical world but also in the world as we wrestle with it. No data seems certain, all boundaries are blurred, and irrationality abounds. To borrow a metaphor from Wittgenstein, the ground is rough—very rough. Hard as we might try, we can never completely bridge the gap between theory and practice. Scientific theory and technology may provide us with various means to extend human life (e.g., the artificial heart), but it does not answer questions concerning when life ought to be prolonged and what counts as a quality life. Science and technology may one day give us the ability to deploy a space-based defensive shield against nuclear attack, but it cannot predict how our adversaries might react to such a development. Would they view such a system as purely defensive, or would they view it as an offensive threat? Would the development of this system have the practical effect of stabilizing or destabilizing international relations? Science cannot give us a final solution to these essentially moral questions because scientific knowledge is not like moral knowledge. In fact, assert post-analytic philosophers, scientific theory and technology offer a cure to our moral problems that often is worse than the disease.

Now how does all this discussion of theory, technology, and practice relate to epistemology and the issue of skepticism? What is the connection? While it may be true that the solutions of scientific theory and technology do, by their very nature, operate with little regard for the many interrelated human practices that they may affect, this does not mean that scientific theory and technology are domains of inquiry that ought to be abandoned. And yet, this is the direction that Gadamer and his adherents seem to be moving towards. His claims concerning the nature of moral knowledge (that scientific theory can never give us moral knowledge) have been applied with equal force to all knowledge. Scientific theory—all theoretical inquiry—cannot provide us with knowledge (at least not the traditional conception of knowledge as opposed to mere opinion). The distinction between moral and scientific knowledge, between value judgments and factual judgments (a distinction which Aristotle took for granted) is seen to have broken down under the force of the skeptic's arguments. Therefore, the lesson to be drawn from Gadamer's observations concerning moral knowledge and practice may be more far-reaching than originally suspected. In the words of Richard Bernstein:

> One must be sensitive to and acknowledge the important differences between the nature of scientific knowledge and other forms of knowledge, but the more closely we examine the nature of this scientific knowledge, the more we realize the character of rationality in the sciences, especially in matters of theory-choice, is closer to those features of rationality that have been characteristic of practical philosophy than to many of the modern images of what is suppose to be the character of genuine *episteme*.[8]

Rorty, as we have seen, is most explicit on this point. He uses Gadamer's view on the primacy of practice over theory to press his own concept of philosophy as edifying discourse rather than systematic theory building. If our best efforts in the realm of theoretical inquiry are in the end based on judgments of value, perhaps we should eschew theory altogether in favor of *phronesis* and *praxis*. Given our need to cope with the practical problems of human life, Rorty urges us to turn away from the search for absolute principles and metaphysical foundations which theoretical philosophy is meant to provide. Instead, we are encouraged to embrace *phronesis* and the practical rather than remain obsessed with the truth and "getting things right" in our theories. Such a recommendation seems especially cogent if theoretical inquiry ultimately leads to skepticism, as I have been arguing. In choosing between edifying philosophy or skepticism, surely edifying philosophy is the lesser of two evils—or is it?

In what remains of this final chapter I want to argue for the following two related points. First, theoretical inquiry, even if it does ultimately lead to some form of skepticism, has a value that edifying philosophy tends to ignore and seems unable to capture. Second, if the end result of theoretical inquiry is skepticism, it is a skepticism that has an important role to play in all our philosophical inquiries, a role that we ought not ignore.

Theory and Practice

Throughout this chapter, and throughout this book, my focus has been on the skeptic's dream possibility and the threat that possibility poses to our knowledge. My emphasis has been on the impossibility of our attaining *certainty* in our beliefs about the world around us. And yet, the skepticism I am advocating has implications which go beyond our inability to attain epistemic certainty. The real lesson of the dream possibility concerns the metaphysical predicament we find ourselves in. The thought that I might be dreaming now dramatically brings home to me my *separation* from the external world. The dream possibility compellingly illustrates the truly *external* nature of the world. It is this separateness, the idea that the world may be (if I am dreaming) nothing like the world I have direct access to, that seems to be the most important implication of skepticism. Skepticism opens up the possibility that we may be completely cut off from the world, and in so doing, it causes us to question our understanding of that world.

What skepticism suggests is that our perspective on the world may be very limited and incomplete. At worst we may always be dreaming, unknowingly trapped in a solipsistic universe. At best we can never be sure when we are dreaming and when we are not, and thus we are never sure if our knowledge of the world is accurate and complete. The lesson of skepticism is that there is no way I can step outside of my own limited perspective and see things as they really are. And yet, if I am to get at the truth, if I am to understand the world as it really is, that is what I need to do. Given this metaphysical bind, a bind that we all find ourselves in, what can we do to satisfy our deeply felt desire to understand the real, external world? Rorty would counsel us to give up the desire as fruitless, and perhaps even pernicious. I would disagree. The desire is neither without merit nor harmful, but to see this we must *maintain* Aristotle's distinction between theory and practice rather than eschew theory in favor of practice.

Despite Hegel's famous dictum, "To abstract is to falsify," I would argue that we need the abstracting power of theory if we are to make any sense of the world. The abstractions of our theories, however incomplete and uncertain they may be, are extremely important in extending our knowledge of the world around us. They allow us to move beyond the particulars of our individual perspective and come to grips with, in some small measure, that which is beyond the boundaries of our finite intellect. Theoretical musings allow us, in some small measure at least, to escape the metaphysical predicament I alluded to earlier. It is a form of inquiry that forces us to imagine the world as it might exist beyond our limited first-person perspective.

Now our theories cannot completely solve the practical problems of everyday living. What makes theoretical inquiry pernicious, and here I agree with Rorty and Gadamer, is thinking that it can. The skeptic is under no such illusion. He recognizes that even our best theories remain uncertain and incomplete. However, theoretical inquiry, and the knowledge it leads to, can and does shed important light on practical problems. To reject theoretical inquiry simply because it always gives us knowledge that is incomplete and somewhat distorted is to reject an avenue of inquiry that is nonetheless extremely valuable—from even a practical point of view. It would be like saying we should reject as worthless all the data received from the Hubble telescope because it is distorted from imperfections on the lenses. We do not reject the data out of hand, but we are circumspect in our use of that data because we recognize its imperfections.

Theoretical knowledge, like the data from the unrepaired Hubble telescope, is not without merit. Our view of the world may be out of focus, but it is the only view we have. We need to make the best of it. One way we make the best of it is through theoretical inquiry. We may not live in a world of frictionless planes, but the theoretical concept of frictionless planes has led to many practical applications in physics and engineering. Similarly, scientific advances in the theories of neonatal medicine will not resolve the disputes over abortion or euthanasia, but they may bring into sharper focus the moral issues that lie at the heart of those disputes. In our ethical theories the realities of human finitude—a reality that skepticism makes clear—dictate against a perfectly rational, all-knowing moral agent, but ethical theories which appeal to the ideals of perfect rationality and certain knowledge are not necessarily bankrupt. In that they tend to isolate certain components of what it means to act in a morally correct manner (e.g., Kant's emphasis on the good will and the utilitarian emphasis on good consequences) they do help us to better understand what is involved in making moral judgments. They yield important insights into how we ought to conduct our lives despite our human frailties. We risk losing these kinds of insights when we believe that practical knowledge alone can be substituted for theoretical knowledge. We need both kinds of knowledge.

Theoretical inquiry often does involve us in a kind of reductionist program. We are taking what appears to be a very rich and complicated reality (the external world) and are trying to understand and explain this reality in a more simplified way—a way that is more amenable to our finite intellect and the limited perspective that intellect entails. Of course when we engage in this kind of reductionism we lose some of the richness and complexity of the external world, but then that was the point. In order for us to get a grasp on this complex world we need to whittle it down to size—our size—making use of the relatively dull knife of our limited intellect. As a result we sometimes shave off more than we want to and sometimes less. However, the reductionism that we engage in when we theorize is not the main culprit here (as Hegel's dictum appears to indicate). Rather it is our epistemic status—a status the skeptical philosopher is well aware of—which makes our reductions incomplete and error-prone. Sure, we end up leaving things out when we theorize; we ignore certain variables or assume, for the sake of theory, that certain variables have a constant value. The perfect theory, complete and devoid of assumptions, is forever beyond our grasp. But as long as we remain cognizant of the incomplete nature of our theoretical abstractions, theoretical knowledge is not so pernicious as edifying philosophy would lead us to believe. In fact, as inquiring human beings, beings who want to find the truth (not just one's own personal truth but the truth all others will subscribe to), it seems we cannot help but abstract and theorize. There is no other way to expand our intellectual horizons.

And yet, if theoretical inquiry aimed at discovering objective truth, especially in the realm of epistemology, seems to lead inexorably to some form of skepticism, why should we not reject theory and the skepticism it entails? Hume sees this as the "chief objection against all *abstract* reasonings." It takes otherwise clear ideas, e.g., our knowledge of the external world, and makes them "seem full of absurdity and contradiction." And because these "absurd opinions are supported by a chain of reasoning the clearest and most natural" we find our reason "thrown into a kind of amazement and suspense."[9] As Ernest Sosa argues, a practicing skeptic finds himself in a sort of "vital incoherence," for as a guide to living, skepticism counsels suspension of belief. But such a suspension of belief is really impossible for any of us to attain. Therefore, none of us can be, in practice, true skeptics.[10]

Michael Williams makes a similar point in his recent work. As he puts it, "sceptical arguments depend essentially on theoretical commitments that are not forced on us by our ordinary ways of thinking about knowledge, justification, and truth."[11] In particular, Williams focuses on the skeptical arguments that make use of the closure principle. As may be recalled from chapter 5, the skeptic makes use of the closure principle in the following manner:

Where p=some claim to knowledge and Sk=some skeptical hypothesis (e.g., the "brain in the vat" hypothesis), assume
(A) S knows p,
(B) S knows (p entails not-Sk), then
(C) S knows not-Sk [from A, B, and the closure principle]. However,
(D) Not-(S knows not-Sk). Therefore,
(E) Not-(S knows p) [from B and D].

Williams accepts the closure principle, but he argues that accepting the truth of D depends on a mistaken commitment to foundationalist theory. The only reason we felt compelled to accept D is because we cannot rule it out by appeal to our sensory experiences (and those experiences are generally what a foundationalist will appeal to as the basic beliefs which justify all his further claims to knowledge).

Now I am not entirely convinced that foundationalist theory is the culprit here, as Williams claims. In addition, his proposal to replace foundationalist theory with a *contextualist* theory is very similar to the proposals offered by externalists (proposals which I have already argued against at length in chapter

5). However, what I want to draw attention to here is his view that skeptical arguments are not so compelling when viewed from the proper context, that is, when viewed from a context stripped of the theoretical underpinnings (underpinnings that may not be so intuitive as initially supposed) upon which skepticism seems to depend.

Along with Hume, Sosa, and Williams (among others) I find this to be the most telling objection to skepticism. It is an objection for which there is no easy answer. However, in the next section I will try to sketch out what I believe is the only route the skeptic can take in reply to this objection.

Making Sense of the Objective World

There is a sense in which Sosa's charge against skepticism is absolutely correct. Within the realm of practice, suspension of belief is not possible. It is not a real alternative. And if skepticism is not a real alternative, it cannot, or should not, be an especially compelling theory. However, if this is the case, what *practical* role, if any, does theoretical skepticism have to play in our lives? This is a question I will take up in the next section where I discuss the value of skepticism and how to reconcile our theory with our practice. But Sosa's and Williams' objections strike at a deeper issue than this. They are objections at the level of *theory* and not just practice. They are objections that question the very logic of theoretical skepticism.

Thompson Clarke offers very much the same type of objection in his discussion of skepticism.[12] According to Clarke, skeptical doubts may be understood in either a "plain" or "philosophical" way. Understood in a plain way, skeptical doubts pose no real threat to our knowledge. G. E. Moore, when he claims while holding up his hands that here is one hand and here is another, is talking in a plain way. Within the plain context, what I would call the practical context, there is no question of doubt. For Moore to go on and justify his claim by asserting, "I know I am not now dreaming," would seem absurd within this plain context. Yet, these kind of plain assertions do not settle the questions of theoretical skepticism. To adequately address skeptical doubts, we must understand them in a philosophical way, within what I would call the theoretical context. However, once we try to understand these doubts in a philosophical way, claims Clarke, they begin to take on a self-refuting nature. To see this, we need to take a closer look at *doubt*.

Doubts seem to require some sort of object. When we doubt, we doubt *something*. In the case of philosophical skepticism, we have doubts about our knowledge of an objective, external world. But these doubts only make sense if we have some conception of such a world. To put it in terms of the dream possibility, the possibility that I am dreaming now only makes sense if I can conceive of waking up sometime in the future, yet my knowledge of that very possibility is precluded by my inability to ever deny the possibility that I am dreaming. Thus, claims Clarke, if skepticism (understood in the philosophical and not the plain way) were true, it would question the very conception of an objective, external world, a world in which I am not dreaming. But without an objective world to discover, without the possibility that I might someday wake up from this dream, how do we make sense of skeptical doubts? Skeptical doubts only make sense if understood in a plain way, and when understood this way, they pose no real threat to our knowledge, thereby losing their compelling nature.

The incoherence of skepticism would appear to extend deeper than merely to the level of practice. It is a fundamental incoherence at the level of theory. Stroud nicely sums up this point as follows:

> If it is true that the possibility of knowledge of the world must be presupposed by the dream-possibility in order for it to undermine our knowledge in the way it does, that traditional conception [of the objective world] cannot be fully coherent. It cannot be the correct account of how it is possible for us to think about an objective world. To examine how the dream possibility actually works would therefore be to examine the intelligibility of that conception.[13]

The allegation here is that theoretical skepticism seems to refute itself. The claim is that theoretical skepticism makes sense only if it is not true. However, must we have some knowledge of the objective world in order to doubt our knowledge of that world? I believe the answer to that question is no. However, I also believe that the thesis of metaphysical realism must be true for the dream possibility to make sense (and this seems like an affirmative answer to the preceding question). How can these two positions be reconciled?

I think the answer lies in distinguishing *knowing* from *conceiving*. Clarke seems to want to claim that in order to conceive of something (the objective world, the dream possibility), we must have some knowledge of that thing. He sees the skeptic's conception of the objective world as presupposing some knowledge of that world, a knowledge which of course the skeptic denies we have. Essentially Clarke is applying Meno's paradox to objects of doubt rather than knowledge.[14] However, this presumes a closer connection between knowing and conceiving than is correct. We seem able to conceive of many things which we know nothing about. I can conceive of forms of life existing in some distant galaxy, but I know nothing about what form this life might take. Along with John Locke, I can conceive of primary substance as that pure substance which supports the qualities we perceive in things, even though I know nothing of that primary substance. Contrary to Clarke, conceiving *p* does not entail knowing anything about *p*, aside from assuming it might exist.

However, before we can doubt something, it does seem clear that we must have some conception of what it is we doubt. In other words, we must *conceive* of *p* before we can *doubt p*. That is what I meant earlier when I claimed that doubts require some sort of object, and that is why I believe the thesis of metaphysical realism must be true for skepticism to make sense. The truth of metaphysical realism gives us something to doubt. We must at least be able to conceive of an objective, external world if the skeptic's doubts are to seem at all compelling. Once the skeptic turns his arguments on the thesis of metaphysical realism in such a way as to make that thesis inconceivable, he has gone too far, as Clarke's arguments make clear. At that point skeptical theorizing does seem self-refuting in much the way that relativism seems self-refuting. Everything is open to doubt, including skepticism. The question is, by what license does theoretical skepticism pull up short of doubting the truth of metaphysical realism? Has the skeptic merely traded one kind of incoherence for another?

In a way the answer is yes. The theoretical skeptic can doubt everything short of doubting that there is an objective truth, a truth which embodies the external world as it *really* is. To doubt the truth of metaphysical realism is to start down the path of the post-analytic program of edifying philosophy and the relativism it entails. I can only hope I have already shown the error of that program: better to embrace skepticism, even if there is a certain incoherence to it. What all this demonstrates (as I pointed out and argued for in chapters 2 and 3) is that even skepticism is ultimately dependent on some sort of underlying presupposition, namely, the truth of metaphysical realism.

Of course Clarke would argue that we are right back where we started. Philosophical skepticism is seen to rely on a conception of the objective, external world which it cannot sustain. Despite everything I have said, I have not really addressed this objection. How is it possible to *conceive* of something which you *know* nothing about? The skeptic says it is possible; Clarke demands to know how.

The only way we can conceive of something we know nothing about is in terms of how that something, in this case the objective, external world, *might be known* by us. Of course in fleshing out this idea of how we might come to know the objective world, we are somewhat limited by what we have already experienced.[15] Nonetheless, we seem to have plenty of examples of how this objective world might be conceived. We might cite Plato's Allegory of the Cave in *The Republic*, with his example of climbing up out of the world of sensibility and into the realm of pure forms and perfect ideas. Or we could resort to something like a God's-eye view of the universe, a view which takes in all perspectives or is perhaps without any perspective (although I confess that this latter possibility, what Thomas Nagel calls "a view from nowhere," is difficult for me to conceive). In any case it is examples like these that help the skeptic to illustrate and make intelligible—in a word, *conceive*—the idea of an objective world, while claiming no direct knowledge of that world. An objection still might be raised concerning these examples. Because theoretical skepticism is seen to depend on some fanciful story about a mysterious, obscure realm called the objective world, how respectable a doctrine can skepticism hope to be? Three replies seem available to the skeptic.

First, the concept of the objective world is not as mysterious and obscure as might be made out. In fact, before it was subject to the skeptic's arguments, it seemed like a pretty straightforward concept, one that many non-skeptical theorists make use of as well. Second, the skeptic has reached his ultimate destination when he gets to these fanciful stories. In many ways this is the whole point of skepticism. In the end all our theories of knowledge, to include skepticism, are seen to rely on some sort of presupposition as a foundation. By coming to realize what these various presuppositions are, we learn something about human knowledge and the limits of that knowledge. As far as presuppositions go, the belief that there is an objective truth about the world to be discovered seems like a pretty tame one to me (even if it ultimately leads to skepticism). This is particularly true when we look at the alternative to this presupposition—that there is *no* objective truth about the world which is the object of our inquiries. This consideration leads to the skeptic's third reply.

In pursuing our inquiries it seems we must all eventually face the following choice. Either we must learn to live with the idea that there is no foundational, unifying answer to the fundamental questions we ask (and all the relativism and chaos that seems to entail) or we must postulate, as a theoretical construct at least, that there is a truth to be discovered, even though that truth always eludes us. The first half of this disjunct—that there is no absolute, objective truth for us to discover but only a kind of relativistic truth—seems awfully difficult to accept. Our passion to seek after universal, foundational answers to the kinds of fundamental questions philosophy poses for us (a passion Camus recognizes and explores in "The Myth of Sisyphus") cannot be denied, even when it leads, as Camus supposed it must, to absurdity. The "examined life" prescribed by Socrates largely consists of following this passion of ours. We want to make universal claims; we want to discover a foundation for our knowledge; we want to find the truth. That's what motivates our inquiries in the first place—the quest for truth. Besides, the search for objective truth, even if never-ending, is not without reward.

Theoretical knowledge, despite the fact that our choice of theory is value-laden and ultimately involves some presuppositions, is not mere jousting at windmills. Theories intrigue us and are of value because they help us understand our human predicament. The absolutes and sharp divides imposed by theoretical reasoning give us a goal for our inquiries. We may never reach the goals imposed by the demands of theoretical reasoning (questions will always remain; we will always leave something out), but our theories can help us to distill and get a mental handle on our lives much in the way good poetry can distill complicated emotions and concepts to their simplest and, in some ways, most beautiful, form. We may never find the objective truth we are searching for (maybe the most we can hope for is to approach truth asymptotically), but the quest seems to possess some sort of intrinsic goodness. We learn something about ourselves when we engage in the quest, and that brings us to the real value of theoretical reasoning and the skepticism such reasoning entails.

The Value of Skepticism

Skepticism, particularly the theoretical skepticism I am arguing for here, is a greatly misunderstood doctrine. Part of the problem lies in the connotations that have become attached to the word *skepticism*. Skepticism is seen by many as a sort of sinister doctrine that leads one to cynicism, solipsism, and eventually nihilism. Such a view of skepticism wrongly denigrates it as some sort of evil to be routed and overcome. But theoretical skepticism is not the bugbear[16] so many have thought it to be. It should not be feared but embraced, for it is essentially a doctrine of hope.

Theoretical skepticism, the idea that we can never attain absolute, certain knowledge—the whole truth as it were—leaves room for the *possibility* that there is such a truth out there. It gives us hope that there is something more to our inquiries and our lives than a relativistic view of truth would allow. It may be a false hope, as Rorty would claim, but it is a hope that is difficult to deny.

We can never fully grasp the objective truth about our lives and the universe, a truth that goes beyond our limited perspective, but we cannot give up the hope that we may yet grasp some small portion of that truth. Chisholm recognizes this when, in discussing the "problem of the criterion," he makes a distinction between the practical and absolute senses of "ought to believe." We can never know, in the absolute sense, according to him, whether we "ought to believe" something. The best we can do is "hope that our marks of evidence will also be marks of truth. . . . If the word *hope* as it is used above, does not seem strong enough, one might use *animal faith*."[17] Whether animal faith or hope, theoretical skepticism leaves open, in a way post-analytic philosophy does not, the possibility of our grasping some small measure of the objective truth. That hope alone is enough to fuel the inquiries of philosophy for a long time to come.

This brings us to another value to be found in theoretical skepticism: its motivational quality. As will be recalled, this was touted as one of the advantages of edifying philosophy over traditional philosophy—it keeps the conversation of mankind going. Traditional philosophy, with its penchant for universal, absolute claims, is seen as a threat to continued conversation and dialogue. After all, once the traditional philosopher has discovered the truth (or at least his version of the truth), what could be the point of further discussion?

But this mistakes the position the traditional philosopher finds herself in. She is never able to claim, as I hope my skeptical arguments have demonstrated, that she has discovered the complete, objective truth. Questions of epistemic justification and metajustification always remain. And because these questions always remain, the discourse of philosophical inquiry continues. The skeptical arguments which pose these questions and doubts are the greatest motivators of philosophical inquiry of all. They continue to intrigue us, puzzle us, and confound us, despite over 2,000 years of philosophical dialogue. Inquiry begins with doubt and will continue as long as that doubt persists. And that doubt will continue to persist as long as we grasp the greatest insight that skepticism has to offer to us—our separateness.

Stanley Cavell, discussing our knowledge of another's pain, eloquently makes this point concerning our separateness:

> But I am filled with this feeling—of our separateness, let us say—and I want you to have it too. So I give voice to it. And then my powerlessness presents itself as ignorance—a metaphysical finitude as an intellectual lack.[18]

And this, as Cavell goes on to assert, is the greatest lesson to be drawn from skepticism. We are trapped in our own perspective, limited by our human finitude. We are forever separated from other minds, cut off from the external world. Yet we cannot help wonder about other minds and the external world. This sense of wonder is really what philosophy is all about; it's how the dialogue of philosophy gets started. The vicissitudes of human life cause us to wonder about our place in the universe. We want to know that world, that *reality*, which lies beyond our limited perspective, even if that quest for objective knowledge is bound to fall short. Still the journey is worthwhile because we learn something important about ourselves: we learn the nature of our metaphysical separateness. The edifying philosopher may view the entire project as quixotic at best, Sisyphean at worst, but I cannot help but believe they do not understand the nobleness and the value inherent in the quest for absolute, objective truth.

But beyond the rather personal and esoteric value of theoretical skepticism to the individual inquirer that I describe above, the question of theoretical skepticism's practical value still bears asking. How *ought* theoretical skepticism affect how we live our lives? *Can* theoretical skepticism affect how we live our lives? It has been argued that, in so far as it is impossible to lead a life where one suspends all of one's beliefs, skepticism cannot affect our lives in any sort of meaningful way. Then, assuming ought implies can, skepticism, especially any kind of skepticism which calls into doubt the vast majority of our ordinary beliefs, *ought* not to play any role in our lives. Sosa's argument against skepticism (the theoretical implications of which I discussed in the previous section) can be seen as taking just such a position within the context of our practical lives. We cannot be true skeptic's because such skepticism leads to a "vital incoherence" at the level of practice. Because of the vital incoherence inherent in skepticism, we have at least a prima facie, practical argument for why we ought not to adopt the skeptic's conclusions.[19]

Instead of embracing the incoherence of skepticism, argues Sosa, we need to take a "perspectival" approach to knowledge, what he calls "virtue perspectivism." The virtue component of Sosa's theory comes about from his view that epistemic justification is somehow connected to intellectual virtue: "A skill or ability that enables one to cope in a cognitively effective way."[20] Some examples of intellectual virtue might include a love of truth, impartiality, careful observation skills, intellectual courage, etc.—in general, exercising a conscientious attitude in the formulation of one's beliefs. Roughly speaking, Sosa argues that knowledge is a matter of appropriately exercising one's intellectual virtues in the formation of beliefs (i.e., exercising these virtues correctly given the field of inquiry and environment one finds himself in) such that when one forms beliefs in this way, these beliefs are very likely to be true.[21] On his view, knowledge depends on both external factors (one's environment) and internal factors (one's inner nature/intellectual virtue).

In some respects, Sosa's theory shares a great deal in common with Plantinga's externalist/naturalistic theory discussed in chapter 5. Like Plantinga, Sosa sees the need for an external/objective component to knowledge (i.e., the knower's environment, a large part of which is the knower's social community) as well as an internal/subjective component (i.e., the knower's inner nature, which is in part formed by the environment).[22] If one has been "persistently successful"[23] in using certain intellectual virtues within a specified field of inquiry and environment, then when one uses those virtues in that field and environment to arrive at beliefs, in all likelihood one has knowledge. For example, my perceptual belief that the rain is beating against my office window counts as knowledge because I have an inner nature (consisting of a certain conscientious attitude in the field of forming perceptual beliefs) and I am in a kind of environment (e.g., I am not dreaming, I am not being manipulated by an evil demon, etc.) such that my beliefs, when I am in *these circumstances*, are frequently true.

Now if I am in *other circumstances*, perhaps subject to one of the skeptical alternatives, I am no longer justified in my beliefs and do not have knowledge. However, Sosa argues that the circumstances we generally find ourselves in are such that we are not subject to the skeptical alternatives. We live in the real world, not the dream world or the demon world. Our intellectual virtues, our standards of justified belief, should be relative to the former and not the latter. The world of theoretical skepticism, with its dream worlds and evil demon worlds, is incoherent at the level of practice and need not generally be considered.

However, Sosa is still left with a considerable challenge. I would agree that intellectual virtue need not, and should not, be tied to the skeptical alternatives world. Even if one is being manipulated by an evil demon and therefore subject to all manner of error in forming beliefs, as long as one is using their intellectual and perceptual faculties as a conscientious reasoner would, it seems to make sense to say that those beliefs are virtuously formed. But this still begs the question of how we determine what constitutes virtuous belief acquisition. Who does the evaluation here? Is that evaluation subject to further evaluation? Why should intellectual virtue be relative to the nonskeptical world? How do we know which world we actually occupy, either as possible knowers or as evaluators of others' knowledge? We seem to be back to the same problem that plagued Goldman and Nozick in chapter 5. Who determines the standards (e.g., the right J-rules) and how do they make this determination?

Stewart Cohen, like Sosa, takes issue with skepticism in much the same manner.[24] According to Cohen, what counts as knowledge (what he calls "our attributions of knowledge") is relative to the context of that attribution. This context is in turn indexed to one's community and its norms or some other standard *intended* by the attributor. Other standards of attribution, such as the ideal standard of the skeptic, may not be relevant. The problem is determining what standard is relevant for our everyday knowledge attributions. Cohen claims that the probability of the skeptical alternative holding—I am now dreaming— is very low. Given the low probability of the skeptical alternative, it is not generally relevant to our attributions of knowledge. It is an alternative we generally need not consider, especially at the level of our everyday knowledge attributions.

There are a number of difficulties with this relevant alternatives approach to skepticism. For one thing, why should the relevance of an alternative depend on its probability? The probability that I will be involved in an automobile accident today is very slight, but I will still buckle my seat belt when I am operating my car. And even if probability should determine relevance, how do we measure this probability?[25] Nonetheless, Cohen's claim (and Sosa's) that the skeptical alternative is not relevant to our everyday attributions of knowledge has some intuitive appeal. Hume, in discussing the merits of theoretical skepticism, makes a similar point about applying skeptical principles to our practical life. The skeptic's arguments

> may flourish and triumph in the schools. . . . But as soon as they leave the shade, and by the presence of the real objects, which actuate our passions and sentiments, are put in opposition to the more powerful principles of our nature, they vanish like smoke.[26]

Hume's advice to the skeptic: He should "keep within his proper sphere," viz., the theoretical sphere.[27]

This, I think, is generally good advice. While skepticism thrives in the theoretical realm, it is not entirely practical as a guide to living one's life. Sosa's and Cohen's views on the incoherence and irrelevance of skepticism within the realm of practice is not to be rejected out of hand. In living our lives we *do* have to entertain beliefs of many sorts—not the least of which are our beliefs concerning the nature of the external world. However, these necessities of practical living do not touch the arguments of theoretical skepticism. Nor do they argue for rejecting theoretical reasoning, and the skeptical conclusions that reasoning leads us to, as completely without practical merit. While it is not practically possible to live one's life in a state of complete, or near complete, skepticism, there is no reason why theoretical skepticism cannot and should not play some role in informing and guiding our practice. This role goes beyond the part skepticism plays in motivating philosophical inquiry. Skepticism also can, and should, guide all our judgments—especially our moral judgments.

It is here, within the realm of moral reasoning that skepticism can have its most salutary effect. If the skeptic can call into doubt our knowledge of the external world, knowledge which we ordinarily view as firmly grounded and unproblematic, how much less sure ought that make us of our knowledge of moral truths. If theoretical skepticism gives one reason to doubt something as obvious as that the sheet of paper upon which this is written is real and not merely the object of a dream, how certain can we be concerning the truth of, for example, Kant's categorical imperative? The point is, we ought never to rest easy in the comfort of *knowing the truth*. Whatever truth we are capable of grasping, to include skepticism, ultimately rests on something other than a solid foundation. The foundation of all *our* knowledge is ultimately our own limited perspective.

This is the great insight that Socrates first gave to philosophy: we do not know as much as we think. Socrates knew more than most, only because he recognized his knowledge of justice, virtue, wisdom, etc. was uncertain and incomplete. This is the same insight that theoretical skepticism provides us. It counsels against extreme dogmatism and for a measure of tolerance in making the practical judgments that guide our lives. As Hume puts it,

> there is a degree of doubt, and caution, and modesty, which, in all kinds of scrutiny and decision, ought for ever to accompany a just reasoner.[28]

This is not to say we must suspend all judgments of truth. We can and must make decisions which we regard, for all practical purposes, as absolutely and universally true or correct, but this must not blind us to the possibility that we may one day discover we are wrong. And this ought not to surprise us! Our metaphysical predicament, our *separateness* from other people and the external world, assures us that we will never discover, with certainty, the *complete* truth.

The attempt to move beyond this limited perspective of ours and discover the complete, objective truth is really what philosophical inquiry is all about. However, because of our metaphysical finitude, our philosophical inquiries require innovative and imaginative thinking. In the end, they require a creative intellectual leap of some sort. Such a creative leap will involve some measure of story-telling, myth, hope, or faith. But once we understand the stories, the myths, and the hopes upon which our version, or our culture's version, of the truth is based, we will have indeed come a long way down the path of philosophical inquiry in search of the complete, objective truth.

Notes

1. Aristotle, *Nichomachean Ethics*, trans. J. A. K. Thomson (New York: Penguin Books, 1976) I139a1–2 (204).

2. Aristotle, *Nichomachean Ethics*, I139a10–15 (204).

3. Aristotle, *Nichomachean Ethics*, I139b13–36 (206–7).

4. Aristotle, *Nichomachean Ethics*, I140a1–23 (208).

5. Aristotle, *Nichomachean Ethics*, I140a24–b30 (209–10).

6. Hans-Georg Gadamer, "Hermeneutics and Social Science," *Cultural Hermeneutics* 2, 1975, 312, as quoted in Richard Bernstein, *Beyond Objectivism and Relativism* (Philadelphia: University of Pennsylvania Press, 1985), 39.

7. Gadamer, *Truth and Method*, 286–87.

8. Richard J. Bernstein, *Beyond Objectivism and Relativism* (Philadelphia: University of Pennsylvania Press, 1985), 47.

9. David Hume, *An Enquiry Concerning Human Understanding*, ed. Eric Steinberg (Indianapolis: Hackett Publishing Co., 1977), 107–8.

10. Ernest Sosa, "The Skeptic's Appeal," in *Knowledge and Skepticism*, ed. M. Clay and K. Lehrer (Boulder, Colo.: Westview Press, 1989), 51–68 (see especially 62–68).

11. Michael Williams, *Unnatural Doubts: Realism and the Basis of Scepticism* (New York: Blackwell, 1991), 31–32.

12. Thompson Clarke, "The Legacy of Skepticism," *The Journal of Philosophy* 69 (November 1972): 754–769.

13. Barry Stroud, *The Significance of Philosophical Scepticism* (New York: Clarendon Press, 1984), 273.

14. Plato, *Meno*, in *Five Dialogues*, trans. G. M. A. Grube (Indianapolis: Hackett Publishing Co., 1981) (80), 69. Clarke's point seems to be that in order to doubt some knowledge claim we must already *know* something about what it is we doubt. But how is this knowledge possible if skepticism is true.

15. Here I am thinking along the lines of Hume's distinction between *impressions* and *ideas*. Our conception or *idea* of the objective world will necessarily be limited by our sensible *impressions* of that world—*impressions* which of course may not represent the world as it really is. See *An Enquiry Concerning Human Understanding*, section II, 9–13.

16. Daniel Dennett, *Elbow Room* (Cambridge: MIT Press, 1984), chapter 1, talks of the problem of free will as being a sort of "bugbear" or "bogeyman" illicitly constructed by philosophers to motivate one's belief that the problem is real and needs to be overcome. His advice on this matter: Don't feed the bugbears.

17. Roderick Chisholm, *Perceiving* (Ithaca, N.Y.: Cornell University Press, 1957), 37–39.

18. Stanley Cavell, *Must We Mean What We Say?* Cambridge: Cambridge University Press, 1976. 263.

19. Sosa, "The Skeptic's Appeal," 62–68.

20. Sosa, *Knowledge in Perspective* (Cambridge: Cambridge University Press, 1991), 270.

21. See chapters 13 and 16 of *Knowledge in Perspective* for the details of Sosa's views in this regard.

22. These two components are roughly identical to Plantinga's distinction between warrant and justification.

23. This is the terminology used most often by Sosa. Presumably he means by this phrase that there is a high frequency of our beliefs being true.

24. See Stewart Cohen's "Knowledge and Context" (*The Journal of Philosophy* 83 [October 1986]: 574–83) and "How to be a Fallibilist" (*Philosophical Perspectives*, vol. 2, ed. James Tomberlin [Atascadero, Calif.: Ridgeview Publishing Co., 1988], 91–123).

25. Even Cohen recognizes this as a problem. See "Knowledge and Context," 584–85.

26. Hume, *An Enquiry Concerning Human Understanding*, section XII, 109–10.

27. Ibid.

28. Hume, *An Enquiry Concerning Human Understanding*, section XII, 111.

Bibliography

Aristotle. *Metaphysics*. In *The Complete Works of Aristotle*. Ed. Jonathan Barnes. Princeton: Princeton University Press, 1984.
———. *Nichomachean Ethics*. Trans. J.A.K. Thomson. New York: Penguin Books, 1976.
Alston, William. "An Externalist's Internalism." *Synthese* 74 (March 1988): 264–83.
———. "Concepts of Epistemic Justification." *The Monist* 68 (January 1985): 57–89.
Ayer, Alfred J. *Language, Truth, and Logic*. New York: Dover, 1952.
———. *The Central Questions of Philosophy*. London: Weidenfeld and Nicholson, 1973.
———. *The Problem of Knowledge*. New York: Penguin, 1956.
———. *Freedom and Morality and Other Essays*. Oxford: Clarendon Press, 1984.
Berkeley, George. *Three Dialogues Between Hylas and Philonous*. In *Principles, Dialogues, and Philosophical Correspondence*. Ed. Colin Turbayne. New York: McMillan Publishing Co., 1987.
Bernstein, Richard J. *Beyond Objectivism and Relativism*. Philadelphia: University of Pennsylvania Press, 1985.
BonJour, Laurence. *The Structure of Empirical Knowledge*, 1–91. Cambridge: Harvard University Press, 1985.
Camus, Albert. "The Myth of Sisyphus." In *The Myth of Sisyphus and Other Essays*. New York: Vintage Books, 1955.
Cavell, Stanley. *The Claim of Reason*. Oxford: Oxford University Press, 1979.
———. *Must We Mean What We Say?* Cambridge: Cambridge University Press, 1976.
Chisholm, Roderick. *Perceiving: A Philosophical Study*. Ithaca, N.Y.: Cornell University Press, 1957.
———. *The Foundations of Knowledge*. Minneapolis: University of Minnesota Press, 1982.
———. *Theory of Knowledge*. 2nd ed. Englewood Cliffs, N.J.: Prentice-Hall, 1977.
Clarke, Thompson. "The Legacy of Skepticism." *The Journal of Philosophy* 69 (November 1972): 754–769.
Cohen, Stewart. "Knowledge and Context." *The Journal of Philosophy* 83 (October 1986): 574–83.

————. "How to be a Fallibilist." In *Philosophical Perspectives*, Vol. 2. Ed. James Tomberlin, 91–123. Atascadero, Calif.: Ridgeview Publishing Co., 1988.

Connolly, John M. and Keutner, Thomas, eds. *Hermeneutics Versus Science? Three German Views.* Notre Dame, Ind.: University of Notre Dame Press, 1988.

Davidson, Donald. "The Myth of the Subjective." In *Relativism: Interpretation and Confrontation.* Ed. Michael Krausz, 159–72. Notre Dame, Ind.: University of Notre Dame Press, 1989.

————. "On the Very Idea of a Conceptual Scheme." In *Post-Analytic Philosophy.* Ed. John Rajchman and Cornell West, 129–43. New York: Columbia University Press, 1985.

Dennett, Daniel C. *Elbow Room.* Cambridge: MIT Press, 1984.

Descartes, René. *Meditations on First Philosophy.* Trans. Donald Cress. Indianapolis: Hackett Publishing Co., 1979.

Dewey, John. *Logic, The Theory of Inquiry.* New York: Holt & Co., 1938.

Dummett, Michael. *Truth and Other Enigmas.* Cambridge: Harvard University Press, 1978.

Flew, Antony. *A Dictionary of Philosophy.* 2nd ed. New York: St. Martin's Press, 1979.

Forgie, J. William. "Wittgenstein, Skepticism, and Non-Inductive Knowledge." *Pacific Philosophical Quarterly* 67 (October 1986): 269–78.

Gadamer, Hans-Georg. *Truth and Method.* Trans. G. Barden and J. Cumming. New York: Crossroad, 1988.

————. "On the Circle of Understanding." In *Hermeneutics Versus Science? Three German Views.* Ed. John Connolly and James Keutner, 68–78. Notre Dame, Ind.: University of Notre Dame Press, 1988.

Gettier, Edmund L. "Is Justified True Belief Knowledge?" In *Knowing.* 2nd ed. Ed. Michael Roth and Leon Galis, 35–38. Lanham, Md.: University Press of America, 1984.

Goldman, Alvin. "Discrimination and Perceptual Knowledge." *The Journal of Philosophy* 73.20 (1976): 771–791.

————. *Epistemology and Cognition.* Cambridge: Harvard University Press, 1986.

————. "Strong and Weak Justification." In *Philosophical Perspectives,* Vol. 2. Ed. James Tomberlin, 51–69. Atascadero, Calif.: Ridgeview Publishing Co., 1988.

————. "Precis and Update on *Epistemology and Cognition.*" In *Knowledge and Skepticism.* Ed. Marjorie Clay and Keith Lehrer, 69–88. Boulder, Colo.: Westview Press, 1989.

Goodman, Nelson. *Ways of Worldmaking.* Indianapolis: Hackett Publishing Co., 1978.

Hanfling, Oswald. *Wittgenstein's Later Philosophy.* Albany: State University of New York Press, 1989.

————. "How Is Scepticism Possible." *Philosophy* 62 (October 1987): 435–53.

Hume, David. *An Enquiry Concerning Human Understanding.* Ed. Eric Steinberg. Indianapolis: Hackett Publishing Co., 1977.

Kant, Immanuel. *Critique of Pure Reason.* Trans. Norman K. Smith. New York: St. Martin's Press, 1965.

————. *Prolegomena to Any Future Metaphysics.* Trans. Lewis White Beck. Indianapolis: Bobbs-Merrill, 1950.

Kuhn, Thomas S. *The Structure of Scientific Revolutions.* 2nd. ed., enlarged. Chicago: University of Chicago Press, 1970.

Locke, John. *An Essay Concerning Human Understanding.* Ed. Alexander C. Fraser.

New York: Dover, 1959.

Malcolm, Norman. "Moore and Ordinary Language." In *The Linguistic Turn.* Ed. Richard Rorty, 111–24. Chicago: University of Chicago Press, 1967.

Moore, George E. *Philosophical Papers.* New York: Humanities Press Inc., 1959.

Nagel, Thomas. *The View From Nowhere.* New York: Oxford University Press, 1986.

Nozick, Robert. *Philosophical Explanations.* Cambridge: Harvard University Press, 1981.

Pappas, George, ed. *Justification and Knowledge.* Dordrecht, Holland: D. Reidel Publishing Co., 1979.

Pastin, Mark. "The Need for Epistemology: Problematic Realism Defended." In *Justification and Knowledge.* Ed. George Pappas, 151–68. Dordrecht, Holland: D. Reidel Publishing Co., 1979.

Plantinga, Alvin. *Warrant: The Current Debate.* New York: Oxford University Press, 1993.

———. *Warrant and Proper Function.* New York: Oxford University Press, 1993.

Plato. *Meno.* In *Five Dialogues.* Trans. G. M. A. Grube. Indianapolis: Hackett Publishing Co., 1981.

———. *Theaetetus.* Trans. Benjamin Jowett. Indianapolis: Bobbs-Merrill/Library of Liberal Arts, 1949.

Pollock, John. *Contemporary Theories of Knowledge.* Totowa, N.J.: Rowman & Littlefield, 1986.

———. *Knowledge and Justification.* Princeton: Princeton University Press, 1974.

———. "A Plethora of Epistemological Theories." In *Justification and Knowledge.* Ed. George Pappas, 93–114. Dordrecht, Holland: D. Reidel Publishing Company, 1979.

Putnam, Hilary. *Reason, Truth, and History.* Cambridge: Cambridge University Press, 1981.

Quine, Willard V. O. *From A Logical Point of View.* Cambridge: Harvard University Press, 1964.

———. *Ontological Relativity and Other Essays.* New York: Columbia University Press, 1969.

Rescher, Nicholas. *The Strife of Systems: An Essay on the Grounds and Implications of Philosophical Diversity.* Pittsburgh: University of Pittsburgh Press, 1985.

———. "Aporetic Method in Philosophy." *Review of Metaphysics* 41 (December 1987): 283–97.

Roth, Michael D. and Leon Galis, eds. *Knowing.* 2nd ed. Lanham, Md.: University Press of America, 1984.

Rorty, Richard. *Contingency, Irony, and Solidarity.* Cambridge: Cambridge University Press, 1989.

———. *Philosophy and the Mirror of Nature.* Princeton: Princeton University Press, 1979.

Russell, Betrand. *The Problems of Philosophy.* Oxford: Oxford University Press, 1959.

Sextus Empiricus. *Outlines of Pyrrhonism.* London: Loeb Classical Library, 1933.

Sosa, Ernest. *Knowledge in Perspective.* Cambridge: Cambridge University Press, 1991.

———. "Beyond Skepticism, to the Best of Our Knowledge." *Mind* 97 (April 1988): 153–88.

———. "Serious Philosophy and Freedom of Spirit." *The Journal of Philosophy* 84 (December 1987): 707–726.

―――. "The Skeptic's Appeal." In *Knowledge and Skepticism*. Ed. Marjorie Clay and Keith Lehrer, 51–68. Boulder, Colo.: Westview Press, 1989.

Stroud, Barry. *The Significance of Philosophical Scepticism*. New York: Clarendon Press, 1984.

―――. "Understanding Human Knowledge in General." In *Knowledge and Skepticism*. Ed. Marjorie Clay and Keith Lehrer, 31–50. Boulder, Colo.: Westview Press, 1989.

Williams, Michael. *Unnatural Doubts: Realism and the Basis of Scepticism*. New York: Blackwell, 1991.

Wittgenstein, Ludwig. *On Certainty*. Trans. Denis Paul and G. E. M. Anscombe. New York: Harper and Row, 1969.

―――. *Philosophical Investigations*. 3rd ed. Trans. G. E. M. Anscombe. New York: Macmillan Publishing Co., 1958.

―――. *Tractatus Logico-Philosophicus*. Trans. D. F. Pears and B. F. McGuinness. London: Routledge and Kegan Paul, 1961.

Index

About the Author

Jeffrey P. Whitman is an assistant professor of philosophy at Susquehanna University in Selinsgrove, Pennsylvania. A graduate of the United States Military Academy (B.S. 1977) and Brown University (Ph.D. 1991), he was a career Army officer until his retirement from military service in 1995. While in the military he taught philosophy at the United States Military Academy for eight years (1987–1995) before coming to Susquehanna University. He has published numerous articles in such journals as *Public Affairs Quarterly*, *Social Theory and Practice*, and *Teaching Philosophy*.